FUNERAL REGISTER *of the* FIRST PRESBYTERIAN CHURCH OF BELFAST 1712–36

Edited by

JEAN AGNEW

ULSTER HISTORICAL
FOUNDATION

Published 1995
Reprinted 2008
Ulster Historical Foundation
Cotton Court, 30–42 Waring Street
Belfast, BT1 2ED
www.ancestryireland.com
New edition prepared by FPM Publishing

ISBN: 978-0-901905-67-3

Cover and design by Wendy Dunbar

This book has received support from the Cultural Traditions Programme of the Community Relations Council which aims to encourage acceptance and understanding of cultural diversity.

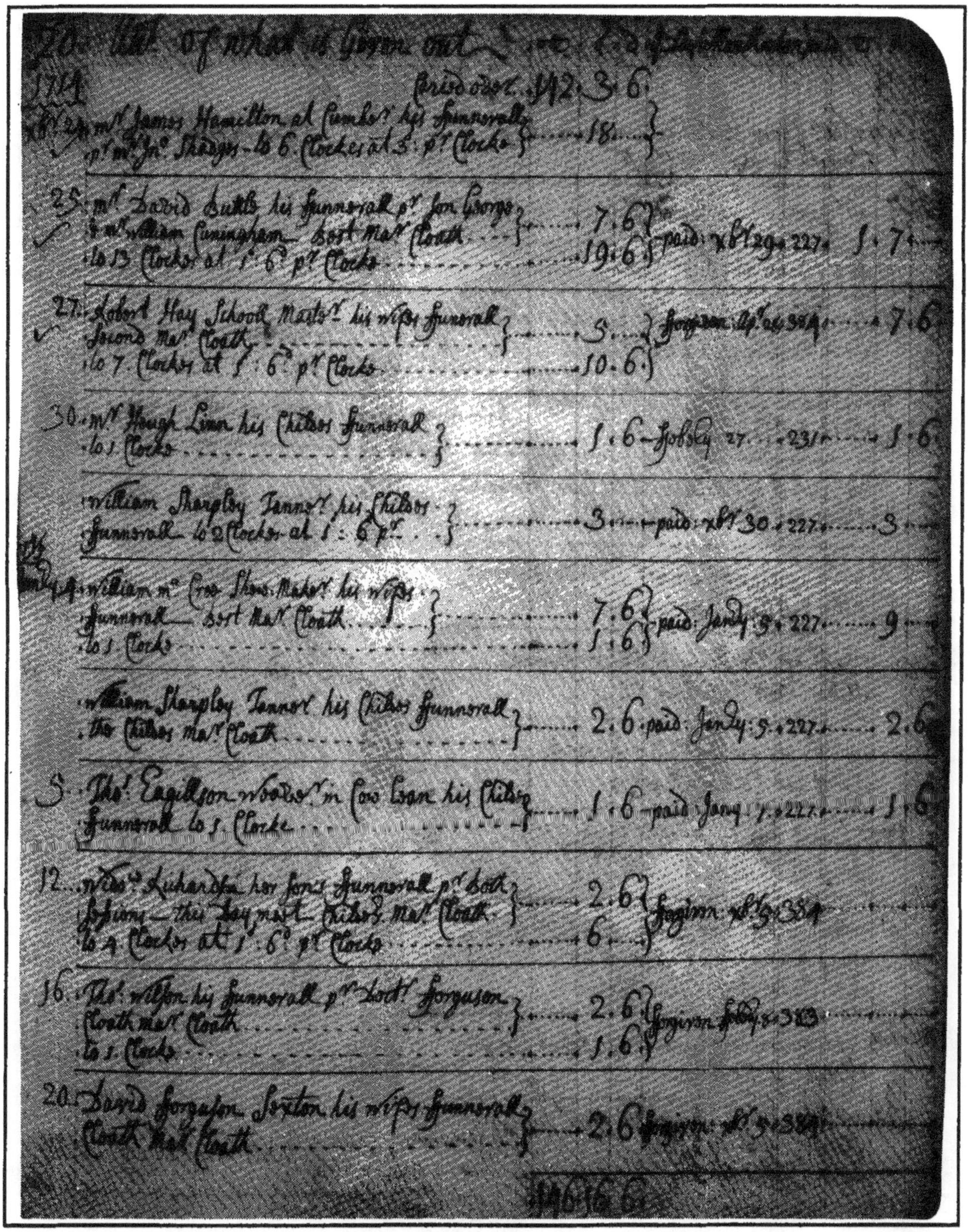

[illegible] of what is given out [illegible]

1714 Carried over 112.3.6

Xbr 24 Mr James Hamilton at [illegible] his ffunnerall pr Mr Jno [illegible] to 6 Clockes at 3 pr Clocke ... 18

25 Mr David Buttle his ffunnerall pr Son George & Mr William Cuningham Best Mar Cloath ... 7.6 / to 13 Clockes at 1s 6d pr Clocke ... 19.6 paid: Xbr 29. 227. 1.7

27 Robert Hay School Master his wifes ffunnerall Second Mar Cloath ... 3 / to 7 Clockes at 1s 6d pr Clocke ... 10.6 fferguson [illegible] 384 ... 7.6

30 Mr Hugh Linn his Childs ffunnerall to 1 Clocke ... 1.6 [illegible] 27 ... 231 ... 1.6

William Sharpley Tanner his Childs ffunnerall to 2 Clockes at 1s 6 pr ... 3 paid: Xbr 30. 227 ... 3

Jany 4 William Mc [illegible] Shoo Maker his wifes ffunnerall Best Mar Cloath to 1 Clocke ... 7.6 / 1.6 paid: Jany 5. 227 ... 9

William Sharpley Tanner his Childs ffunnerall the Childs Mar Cloath ... 2.6 paid: Jany 5. 227 ... 2.6

5 Thos Eagilson Weaver in Cow Lane his Childs ffunnerall to 1 Clocke ... 1.6 paid: Jany 7. 227 ... 1.6

12 Widw Richardson her Sons ffunnerall pr [illegible] this Day next Childs Mar Cloath to 4 Clockes at 1s 6d pr Clocke ... 2.6 / 6 fferguson Xbr 9. 384

16 Thos Wilson his ffunnerall pr Docr fferguson Cloath Mar Cloath to 1 Clocke ... 2.6 / 1.6 fferguson [illegible] 383

20 David fferguson Sexton his wifes ffunnerall Cloath Mar Cloath ... 2.6 fferguson [illegible] 384

146.16.6

25 DECEMBER 1714,
Funeral of David Buttle, who resigned as sovereign of Belfast in 1704
on the passing of the Test Act.

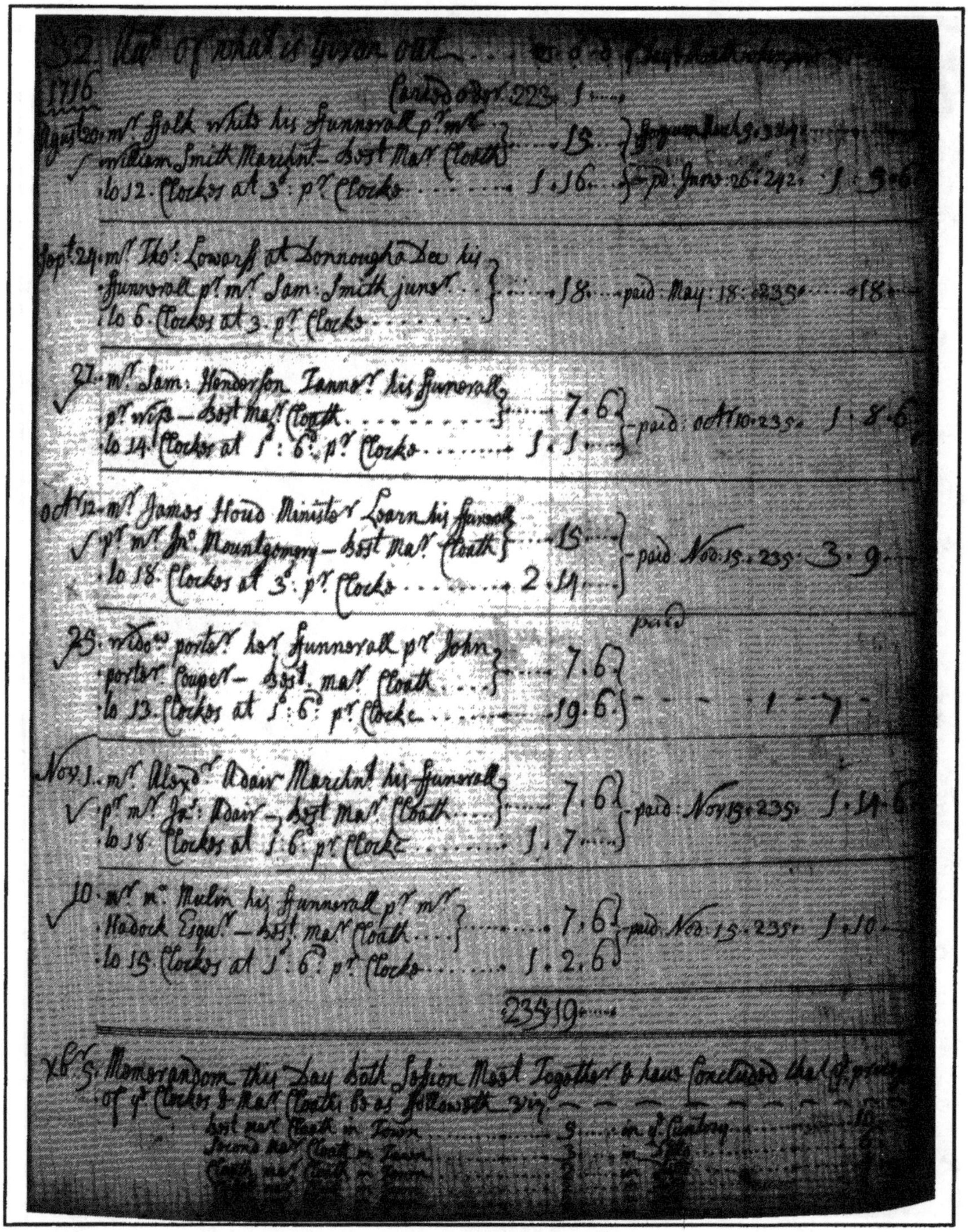

32 Acct of what is Given out ...

1716 Carried over 223 . 1 ...

Agust 20. mr Jolh white his funnerall pr mr william Smith Marchnt — best Mar Cloath ... 15 ...
to 12 Clocks at 3s pr Clocke ... 1 . 16 ... pd June 26 : 242 . 1 : 9 : 6

Sept 24. mr Thos Lowarg at Donnoughadee his funnerall pr mr Sam: Smith junr ... 18 ... paid May 18 : 235 ... 18 ...
to 6 Clocks at 3. pr Clocke

27. mr Sam: Henderson Tanner his funnerall pr wids — best Mar Cloath ... 7 . 6
to 14 Clocks at 1s : 6d pr Clocke ... 1 . 1 ... paid oct 10 : 235 . 1 : 8 : 6

oct 12. mr James Houd Minister Loarn his funerall pr mr Jno Mountgomery — best Mar Cloath ... 15 ...
to 18 Clocks at 3s pr Clocke ... 2 . 14 ... paid Nov 15 : 235 . 3 . 9

25. widow porter her funnerall pr John porter Couper — best mar Cloath ... 7 . 6
to 13 Clocks at 1s 6d pr Clocke ... 19 . 6 ... paid ... 1 . 7

Nov 1. mr Alexdr Adair Marchnt his funnerall pr mr Jas Adair — best Mar Cloath ... 7 . 6
to 18 Clocks at 1s 6d pr Clocke ... 1 . 7 ... paid Nov 15 : 235 . 1 . 14 . 6

10. mr mc Melin his funnerall pr mr Hadock Esqur — best Mar Cloath ... 7 . 6
to 15 Clocks at 1s 6d pr Clocke ... 1 . 2 . 6 ... paid Nov 15 : 235 . 1 . 10

23 . 19 ...

Xbr 5. Memorandom this Day both Session Meet Together & have Concluded that ye price of ye Clocks & Mar Cloaths be as followeth viz
best mar Cloath in Town ... 9 ... in ye Cuntory ... 10
Second Mar Cloath in Town ... 3 ... in ...
Clocks mar Cloath in Town ...

Page written by Thomas Swendill showing the new rates which were introduced in 1716.

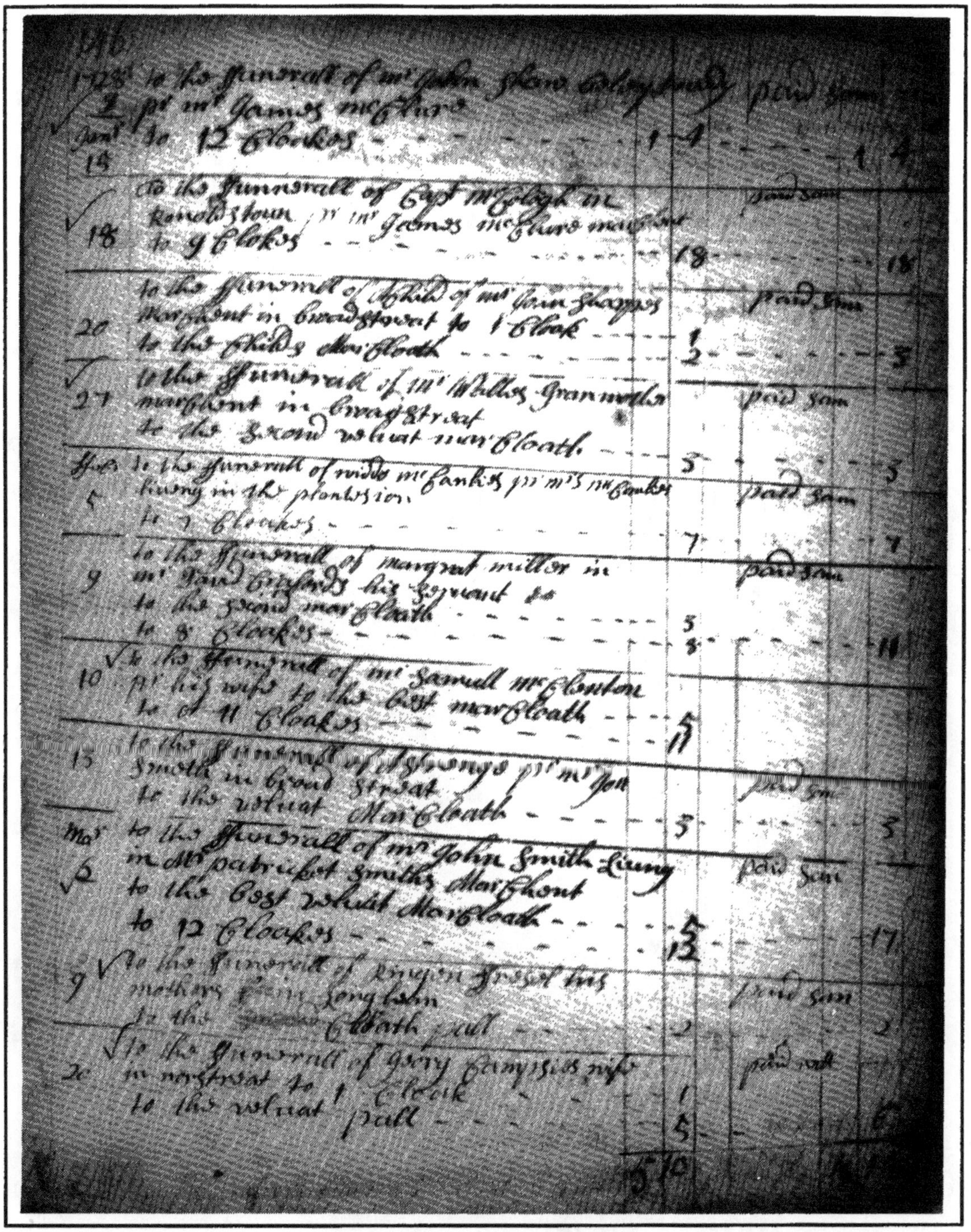

1728 to the ffunerall of mr John [illegible] pr mr James mcClure — paid Sam
Jan. 14 to 12 Cloakes — 1 4 — 1 4
18 to the ffunerall of Capt McCullagh in Ranoldstown pr mr James mcClure marchant to 9 Cloakes — 18 — 18 — paid Sam
20 to the ffunerall of a child of mr John Sharpes Marchant in broadstreet to 1 Cloak to the childs mortcloath — 1 2 — 3 — paid Sam
27 to the ffunerall of mr Wallers Granmother marchant in broadstreat to the second velvet mortcloath — 5 — 5 — paid Sam
ffeb 5 to the ffunerall of widdo mcCanless pr mrs mcCanless living in the plantation to 7 Cloakes — 7 — 7 — paid Sam
9 to the ffunerall of margret miller in mr Paul Crafords his servant to the second mortcloath to 8 Cloakes — 5 8 — 11 — paid Sam
10 to the ffunerall of mr Samuell mcClinton pr his wife to the best mortcloath to 11 Cloakes — 5 11
15 to the ffunerall of [illegible] pr mr [illegible] Smith in broad street to the velvet mortcloath — 5 — 5 — paid Sam
Mar 6 to the ffunerall of mr John Smith living in mr patrick Smiths marchant to the best velvet mortcloath to 12 Cloakes — 5 12 — 17 — paid Sam
9 to the ffunerall of [illegible] his mothers in [illegible] to the [illegible] Cloath pall — 2 — 2 — paid Sam
20 to the ffunerall of [illegible] wife in northstreat to 1 Cloak to the velvet pall — 1 5 — 6 — paid [illegible]
5 10

Page written by Samuel Pentland

CONTENTS

INTRODUCTION

The funeral register of Rosemary Street Presbyterian Church has been known to local historians and genealogists for well over a century. It was printed in 1887 as part of a work entitled *Historic Memorials of the First Presbyterian Church of Belfast* and had already been used by George Benn for his second edition of the *History of Belfast* (Belfast, 1877). It was printed as an exact transcript of the original, without an index, and consequently has been very difficult to use. The funeral register is the most important single source for family history research in Belfast in the early eighteenth century. It runs from 1712 to 1736, ending just before the foundation of the *Belfast Newsletter*, which carried notices of some marriages and deaths, and nine years before the start of the earliest surviving parish register for Belfast. The Ulster Historical Foundation is bringing out this new edition of the 1887 transcript, complete with an index and notes on some of the more important people listed, in order to make the register more widely known and more accessible.

The First and Second Rosemary Street Presbyterian Congregations owned a collection of palls, cloaks and hats which they hired out for funerals. They were used by most of the better-off inhabitants of Belfast, regardless of religion, and by many of the gentry, clergy and substantial farmers in the surrounding countryside even as far away as Counties Londonderry and Tyrone.

The practice of owning 'mort cloths' for hire was common in presbyterian churches in Scotland. The earliest known reference to it in Ireland is to be found in the papers of the Montgomery family who settled in Co. Down at the beginning of the seventeenth century. In *The Montgomery Manuscripts* there is a description of the funeral of the first Earl of Mount Alexander in September 1663: 'many followed us . . . in long black cloaks, which they hired in Belfast for that service'. At that date the Belfast presbyterians had no meeting house, and their minister, the Rev. William Keyes, was in exile in Galway as a result of the discovery of Blood's Plot in which he and other presbyterian ministers were suspected of complicity. It is possible, therefore, that this early collection of funeral cloaks belonged to Belfast corporation rather than to the presbyterian congregation. Londonderry corporation owned a similar collection of cloaks and palls in the 1670s.

The earliest direct reference to the Rosemary Street cloaks and palls is to be found in a letter of 2 July 1705 from Isaac Macartney to Henry Maxwell of Finnebrogue, near Downpatrick, about the funeral of Maxwell's grandfather. Macartney was a leading merchant of Belfast who was one of the elders of the First Presbyterian Church, and also a burgess. In addition to the hire of the funeral apparel, he supplied Maxwell with a gallon each of brandy and canary wine. Crepe for hatbands, ribbons, gloves, raisins and almonds, which were returnable if not needed, were supplied by Samuel Smith, another elder. The total bill amounted to £18.1s.6d.

In 1712, when the funeral register began, the town of Belfast had only existed for a little more than one hundred years. Judging by the names in the cess lists of the 1640s, contained in the Town Book, many of the inhabitants at that date would appear to have been of English origin, although a number of Scots presbyterian families are known to have settled in Belfast by then. However, after the Civil War period, the town attracted more settlers from Scotland, and most of these were presbyterians. Many were merchants, and their trading activities greatly increased the importance of the town. In 1685, a Government surveyor described Belfast as '... one of the most considerable places in the kingdom, having never less than forty or fifty of sail of ships before it, the place very numerous ...' and recommended that a citadel with a port be built, and that Carrickfergus Castle be demolished so that the materials could go towards the work at Belfast.

By the 1690s, Belfast had grown into one of the most important ports in Ireland and the centre of the provisions trade for the North. Undeterred by a rather poor harbour – larger vessels had to lie three miles away from the town in the Pool of Garmoyle to be unloaded by gabards or lighters – the Belfast merchants exported salt beef and butter as far east as Bergen and Stockholm, as far west as Virginia and the West Indies, and to many European ports. They also exported hides, tanned leather, tallow, salmon from Coleraine, and herrings from Scotland. Apart from tar and sawn softwoods from Scandinavia, most of the goods imported were luxuries such as wine, brandy, paper, raisins and prunes from France, and tobacco and sugar from the New World.

The first presbyterian meeting house in Belfast is thought to have been built in about 1668 near the North Gate, which was near the junction of North Street and Hercules Street (now Royal Avenue). The first minister, the Rev. William Keyes, soon received a call to the meeting house in Bull Alley, Dublin, and was replaced in 1674 by the Rev. Patrick Adair, author of the *True Narrative of the Rise and Progress of the Presbyterian Government in the North of Ireland.* Adair and his successor, the Rev. John McBride, were two of the most outstanding presbyterian ministers of their day. In about 1694, McBride, who had recently been called to Belfast after Adair's death, prevailed upon the third Earl of Donegall (with whom he was on friendly terms) to grant a plot of land for a new presbyterian meeting house in Rosemary Street (which was then called Rosemary Lane).

From 1695, a combination of poor harvests in Scotland and low rents in Ireland brought a new wave of Scottish immigrants. Within about ten years it had become apparent that the new presbyterian meeting house was too small for the congregation. McBride was in Scotland at this time, having refused to take the Abjuration Oath, but sent his agreement in June 1706 to the dividing of the congregation if it reached a total of 3,000 persons. The elders acted immediately and a new meeting house had already been built next to the old one on the plot in Rosemary Lane before the General Synod gave its formal approval in April 1708. An amicable agreement had been signed by representatives of the old congregation and the new to divide the stipend between McBride and the Rev. James Kirkpatrick who had been in Belfast since 1706 as an assistant in his absence. Like the plate, the funeral equipment was held in common by the two congregations.

By the early eighteenth century the majority of the inhabitants of Belfast were presbyterians and this was reflected in the government of the town. The Belfast corporation consisted of twelve burgesses and a sovereign (or mayor). In the 1680s only two of their number were actually presbyterians, although several others came from families with presbyterian connections. After the accession of William and Mary, and the abrogation of the Oath of Supremacy in 1691, the numbers of presbyterian burgesses increased, reaching a peak of nine, including the sovereign, in 1701. Following the Test Act of 1704, which required office holders to take the sacrament in the established church, the presbyterian sovereign resigned and the remaining presbyterian burgesses were finally ousted in 1707.

The measures to remove the presbyterian burgesses had been set in train by the widowed Countess of Donegall and it is interesting to note that there seems to have been little or no hostility towards them from the Church of Ireland residents into whose hands the control of the town passed. Indeed Nicholas Thetford, a member of one of the oldest Church of Ireland families of Belfast, refused to be elected in 1707 in place of William Craford, one of the presbyterian burgesses, not wanting a burgess-ship 'coming in such a manner'. Presbyterians and conformists united against the Vicar of Belfast when he claimed that the inhabitants of Belfast should pay him a rate known as 'house money' and, in 1713, eighty of the Church of Ireland merchants and traders of Belfast signed a declaration refuting a charge that the presbyterian merchants had ever used unfair practices in only trading amongst themselves.

There were very few Roman catholics in Belfast at the beginning of the eighteenth century. In 1707 the sovereign George Macartney wrote to the Secretary's Office in Dublin 'we have not amongst us within the town above seven papists'. In obedience to a proclamation by the Government and Council he issued a warrant for the arrest of the one popish priest within his jurisdiction. This priest, Father Phelomy O'Hamol of Derriaghy, courteously surrendered himself, but there was such good will towards O'Hamol on the part of the protestant community, many of whose goods he had helped to protect during the Williamite War, that they offered to pay his bail.

In 1712, when the register begins, Belfast was still a small town extending to the north no further than Smithfield, to the west to the top of Peter's Hill and to the end of Mill Street (now Divis Street), and to the south as far as Ann Street which led to the Long Bridge over the Lagan where the Queen's Bridge is today. Four years previously Belfast Castle, the residence of the Chichester family, had been gutted by fire, apparently by the carelessness of a servant. Three young sisters of the fourth Earl of Donegall died in the blaze. The entrance to the castle grounds was at the top of the Cornmarket where it joins High Street. The castle had been surrounded by gardens which were admired by William III on his visit to Belfast in June 1690, *en route* to the Boyne, and which were developed as building land after the destruction of the Castle.

The original Town Quay was where the River Farset drained into the Lagan (more or less beneath the site of the Albert Clock), and the Farset ran open down the middle of the High Street, crossed by several bridges, the most important of which, the Stone Bridge, was opposite Bridge Street. Between 1715 and 1719, Isaac Macartney reclaimed a piece of wasteland at the mouth of the Farset, making two new quays, George Quay and Hanover Quay, situated on the south side of the modern Queen's Square and along the line of present day Oxford Street (the present embankment not being built until the nineteenth century). He also made a small property development with two main streets, Marlborough Street and Prince's Street.

The merchant community, which in the seventeenth century had dealt largely in provisions, was now able to export large quantities of fine quality linen, the development of the manufacture of which had been encouraged by the settlement of Quaker families from Yorkshire around Moyallon and Lurgan, Co. Armagh, in the 1650s, and by the Huguenots at Lisburn from the 1690s.

In 1721 a third presbyterian meeting house was founded, but there was no separate burying ground for presbyterians in Belfast until the nineteenth century. Most of the people listed in the funeral register would have been buried in the graveyard of the Corporation Church in the High Street. The Corporation Church fell into disrepair in the eighteenth century, and having become structurally dangerous was pulled down in 1774. The new parish church of St Anne (on the site of the present cathedral) was started in that year and completed in 1776, the episcopalian congregation worshipping in the meantime in one of the presbyterian meeting houses in Rosemary Lane. Increasing embankment and dredging to improve the harbour had made the Farset, which at that date was still open at the east end of the High Street, more tidal and the churchyard was occasionally flooded. When the New (Clifton Street) Burying Ground was opened, burials in the old graveyard were forbidden as a public nuisance. The graveyard remained in a ruinous and overgrown state for a few more years until the present St. George's Church was built over it. Most unfortunately no record was made of the gravestone inscriptions before the graveyard was obliterated, and the only fragment which remains is a part of the Pottinger family monument which was removed to Kilmore, Co. Down, in 1813.

THE REGISTER

The register contains details of about 2,000 funerals, each entry giving the place of residence and occupation of the person concerned. The entries generally name the head of the family and his relationship to the person being buried, e.g. 'Mr James Reed apothecary his child's funeral'. Children and wives are never named and ages are not given. Then follows the name of the person paying for or arranging the funeral, e.g. '1712 Aug 12 Mr Goudy, Minister, Ballywalter, his son's funeral, per Mr John Clugston'. Gentry, clergy and well-to-do townsmen were usually called 'Mr'. Unmarried ladies at this date were always called 'Mrs', often followed by their christian name. If the person arranging or paying for the funeral was a relation the register frequently states the relationship. Some of the elders arranged a great number of funerals, acting in an official capacity. Among these are John Chads, John McClure, and Samuel Smith senior, and they are easy to spot because their names appear so many times. Where the hirer of the funeral gear is not an elder and is not named as a relation, further research will often reveal his connection with the person being buried.

There were three qualities of palls or mort cloths, the most expensive being made of velvet. Probably all were trimmed with ribbons and tassels. The velvet palls cost 5s to hire in town, and 10s in the country. All other items were also double in the country, down to cloaks, which cost 2s as against 1s in town. The average cost of hiring equipment for a child's funeral in town was 2-3s. This did not include the coffin. (Labourers at this date were paid about 8d a day.) Hire of palls and cloaks for the most expensive funerals in the country came to between £3 and £4. The largest bills were not necessarily paid for the funerals in the richest families, presumably because many of the gentry families actually owned mourning cloaks and palls and so only needed limited numbers of cloaks from Rosemary Street. A reference to the church's cloaks in the accounts also suggests that the parish church had some to hire.

The charges for hiring cloaks and palls were reduced by about a third at the end of 1716. This was a time of economic recession and the elders may have felt unhappy about charging so much when the initial costs had probably long since been recouped, although small sums were spent from time to time on repairs. The hire of the funeral equipment brought in about £50 a year, but much of this money was probably used for charitable purposes.

The first part of the register, from 1712-18, is written in the clear, educated hand of the sexton, Thomas Swendill. Swendill also recorded payments on several pages at the end of the volume. He was succeeded by David Ferguson, and Ferguson was succeeded in 1720 by Samuel Pentland, who was assisted by William Dick. Most of the latter part of the register is in Pentland's hand. Payments are simply noted 'paid Sam' or 'paid Will'. Every three or four years two of the elders worked through the register listing unpaid debts, many of which, it is noted, were eventually forgiven by the session. These lists of debtors have not been transcribed but photocopies may be consulted at the Public Record Office of Northern Ireland. Very occasionally, they may contain additional information. Pentland's hand is not that of a clerk though it is generally legible. However, because blank pages or parts of pages were used in the late eighteenth or early nineteenth century for domestic accounts, particularly for the purchase of small items of haberdashery, many pages are difficult to decipher.

The main body of the register was transcribed and published in 1887 and this transcription has been reproduced in this volume. The appendix contains some minor addenda and corrigenda but on the whole the transcription is accurate – if a little unforgiving. Pentland wrote a long 'c', dipping below the line of text, which has been transcribed as a capital letter, and a rounded 'v' which has been transcribed as 'u'. The transcriber has used abbreviations (such as 'c' for child, 'm' for mother) in a column after the date to avoid copying out each entry in full. The spelling is wildly original but in defence of the sextons it must be said that they lived in an age when no great store was set by consistent spelling. Much is phonetic – beaker (baker) and gleaser (glazier) are spelt the way they were pronounced. A glossary of trades and occupations and of some of the more unusual place names has been provided. The problems posed by the highly idiosyncratic spelling of surnames is dealt with in the section describing the index (see p.6). If an entry fails to make sense the reader is advised to say it out loud.

Throughout the period covered by the register, in England and Ireland the new year was reckoned to begin on 25 March (Lady Day). Thus 24 March 1714 was followed by 25 March 1715. The modern style of dating the new year from 1 January was not in official use until 1752. The register has been printed with old style dating, as in the original, so care must be taken to ascertain the correct year for funerals between 1 January and 24 March.

THE APPENDIX

The appendix contains biographical notes on many of the notable people in the register arranged in date order of entry. These names appear in the index. Reference numbers are to collections in the Public Record Office of Northern Ireland. The appendix also includes omissions noted when comparing the printed version with the original. Corrections and alternative readings of the original have only been included if significant.

THE INDEX

The eccentricity of the spelling of surnames makes it impossible to index by the names of individuals. Instead the index gathers together groups of variant spellings. For example, Pottinger, Poringer and Podnegar, are all versions of the same name and so are grouped together. The editor cannot guarantee that all groups of surnames relate to the same family but hopes that this method of indexing will make it easier for the user to make identifications. Surnames are indexed each time they actually appear in print, thus 'John Parker, per son John' counts as one reference and 'Widdo Parker, per son John Parker' as two. The index also covers the biographical notes printed in the appendix. Here, if two references are indicated, there are two notes on a particular family on the same page.

ACKNOWLEDGEMENTS

The editor is grateful to the Rev. D. G. Banham for allowing access to the original register and for permission to reproduce pages as illustrations. Thanks are due to the staff of the Ulster Historical Foundation for help in preparing the final text for publication.

J.H.A

BIBLIOGRAPHY

[ ] *Historic Memorials of the First Presbyterian Church of Belfast* (Belfast, 1887)

GEORGE BENN, *A history of the town of Belfast* (Belfast, 1877)

R. S. J. CLARKE (ed.), *Gravestone Inscriptions* (ULSTER HISTORICAL FOUNDATION)

REV. GEORGE HILL (ed.), *The Montgomery Manuscripts 1608-1706* (Belfast, 1869)

J. & S. G. MCCONNELL (eds.), *Fasti of the Irish Presbyterian Church, 1613-1840* (Belfast, 1935)

S. SHANNON MILLIN, *Additional Sidelights on Belfast History* (Belfast & London, 1938)

D. J. OWEN, *History of Belfast* (Belfast & London, 1921)

R. W. M. STRAIN, *Belfast and its Charitable Society* (Oxford, 1961)

R. M. YOUNG, *The Town Book of the Corporation of Belfast* (Belfast, 1890)

GLOSSARY OF TRADES, PROFESSIONS AND OCCUPATIONS

beaker	baker
breaser	brazier
brower	brewer
caper smith	copper smith
car man	carrier
chanler/chanelar/chanlor	chandler
colonneill/cornall/cornel	colonel
couper/cuper/copar	cooper
colectr	collector of customs
cotelar	cutler
corier	currier
cornour/cornnour	coroner
ealseler/elseler/eall selear	ale seller
gabert man	owner or crew member of a gabart, a small boat for unloading ships
gleaser	glazier
glower	glover
gon smith	gun smith
in keper	innkeeper
jurneyman	journeyman
kie porter	docker
leabrower	labourer
maironer	mariner
malster	maltster
marchant	merchant
nealor	nailer
osler	ostler
penter	painter
poater	potter
poathicarry/potegar/potgar	apothecary
prenter	printer
prentise	apprentice
returny/retrny	attorney
ropp macker	rope maker
sargen/surgen	surgeon
seadler	saddler
sealowr	sailor
showmacker	shoemaker
sleater	slater
sope boyler	soap boiler
stashenor	stationer
sufren	sovereign (mayor)
taner	tanner
tealear/tealowr	tailor

tidweater	tidewaiter (customs officer)
tobacco/tobaccow spener	tobacco spinner
truper	trooper
ventnar	vintner
wedo	widow

GLOSSARY OF PLACE NAMES

IN BELFAST

Adem & Eave	Adam & Eve (inn)
browrie	brewery
Cafey house	coffee house
Casel streat	Castle Street
Coawe Hill	? Cave Hill
Egel & Chill	Eagle & Child (inn)
HarClus/harkels/Haklous lean	Hercules Lane
Hanouer Kie	Hanover Quay
Kee/Kie/Keay	Quay
Long Casa	Long Causeway
melon/mellon	Malone
norst/nor street	North Street
pettershill	Peters Hill
plantation/planteson/plant teshen	plantation, area north of Waring Street
Shaes bridg	Shaws Bridge
Shogerhous	Sugar house
sin of the son	Sign of the Sun (inn)
skiper lean/scepers lean	Skippers Lane
slows bridg	Sluice Bridge
stronmilles	Stranmillis
varen street	Waring Street

ELSEWHERE

Ballidrean	Ballydrain, Co. Down
Bangull/banger	Bangor, Co. Down
Belecoan	Ballycowan, Co. Down
Beley Esten	Ballyeaston, Co. Antrim
Beleygoemartin	Ballygomartin, Co. Antrim
Beley Manoh	Ballymena, Co. Antrim
Beleynehinch/beleninch	Ballynahinch, Co. Down
Beliobikin	Ballyobegan, Co. Down
Belliclear/belley Clear	Ballyclare, Co. Antrim
Belliwalter	Ballywalter, Co. Down
Bleariss	Blaris, Co.Down; Blaris parish (Lisburn)
Bosh	Bush, Co. Antrim
Brid eland	Broadisland, Co. Antrim
Carickferguss/careforgous	Carrickfergus, Co. Antrim
Carn castel	Carncastle, Co. Antrim
Caselreah	Castlereagh, Co. Down

GLOSSARY OF PLACE NAMES

Celeleah	Killyleagh, Co. Down
Celenchey	Killinchy, Co. Down
Cellmegen	Kilmegan, Co. Down
Celwaghter	Kilwaughter, Co. Antrim
Cloagh milles	Cloghmills, Co. Antrim
Cnoak	Knock, Co. Down
Cumber	Comber, Co. Down
Curdonall/kerkdonall	Kirkdonald (Dundonald), Co. Down
Dearey	Derry (Londonderry)
Dene goar/Dunegoar/Dinygor/Dunagor	Donegore, Co. Antrim
Dinnean	Duneane, Co. Antrim
Dogh	Doagh, Co. Antrim
Donnougha Dee	Donaghadee, Co. Down
Dun mory	Dunmurry, Co. Antrim
Gelgoram	? Galgorm, Co. Antrim
Gleasrie	Glastry, Co. Down
GlenEavey	Glenavy, Co. Antrim
Helsborow	Hillsborough, Co. Down
Hoalewood/hoolowood/hallewood/Jolewood	Holywood, Co. Down
KeleaD	Killead, Co. Antrim
Learn	Larne, Co. Antrim
Lesnetronk	Lisnatrunk, Co. Down
Mahrehoahel/Mahrihoohel/Marherihall	Ahoghill, Co. Antrim (old name was Magherahoghill)
Mayorah	Moira, Co. Down
Newtoun/nutan/nuttan	Newtownards, Co. Down
port of ffery	Portaferry, Co. Down
Ronaldstown/ronels	Randalstown, Co. Antrim
Sant feield	Saintfield, Co. Down
Skiginearll	Skegoniell, Co. Antrim
Tempell patricket/tampelpatrek	Templepatrick, Co. Antrim

ABBREVIATIONS USED IN THE TRANSCRIPTION

b	brother
c	child
cd	child, daughter
cs	child, son
d	daughter
f	father
gc	grandchild
m	mother
s	son
si	sister
w	wife

FUNERAL REGISTER, 1712–1736

[This book was begun 10th June, 1712, but the page containing the first entries is lost. It contains 171 pages of Funeral Entries (the last being dated 19th October, 1736), and 58 pages of accounts connected with them. The entries to 29th July, 1718, are in the clerkly hand of Thomas Swendill, sexton of the First Congregation, to whose widow eight shillings was paid for the book, on 20th Oct., 1718. Swendill was succeeded as sexton by David Ferguson (till 5th Feb., 1720), and Ferguson by Samuel Pentland (or, as he writes his name, Samull Pentelan). The entries do not give the dates of deaths, but of burials, with an account of the mort cloths (or palls) and cloaks used at the funeral. These funeral trappings were originally the property of the First Congregation, and afterwards the joint property of the First and Second Congregations, and were lent on hire. The entries show that they were often let out for funerals in connection with other congregations, sometimes at considerable distances from Belfast. The following is an exact copy of the earliest extant page, omitting only some later scribblings.]

2.	Acct of what is Given out.	£ s d	ye Day and Month when paid.		£ s d
1712.	Caried over	9 . 12 . 6			
July : 12.	. Bealy Adam's his Wife's ffunnerall . Best Mar Cloath - - - - - - - - . to 1 Clocke - - - - - - - - - -	... 7 . 6 ... 1 . 6	paid : July 21.	219.*	... 9 ...
16.	. mr William White Ship-Carpinter his ffunerall . pr Salt Jno Park—Best Mar Cloath - . to 11 Clockes at 1s: 6d: pr Clocke -	... 7 . 6 ...16 . 6	paid : Janry : 10.	221.	1 . 4 ...
	. mr Jas Reed poathicarrey his Childes ffunnerall . to 1. Clocke - - - - - - - - - -	... 1 . 6	paid : July : 22.	219.	... 1 . 6
21.	. Thos Tayler plantation his ffunnerall . Cloath Mar Cloath - - - - - - -	... 2 . 6	paid : Agust : 4.	219	... 2 . 6
26.	. mr Jas ffarrly Dr his ffunnerall pr mrs mccBride . Best Mar Cloath - - - - - - - - . to 8 Clockes at 1s: 6d: pr Clocke - -	... 7 . 6 ...12 ...	fforgiven : June 15.	383.	....

2.	Acct of what is Given out.	£ s d	ye Day & Month when paid.		£ s d
July 29.	. mr John Anderson Doctr his ffunnerall . Best Mar Cloath - - - - - - - . to 14. Clockes at 1s: 6d: pr Clocke -	... 7 . 6 1 . 1 ...	paid: Agust: 4.	219.	1 . 8 . 6
30.	. Heugh Agnew Couper his ffunnerall . Best Mar Cloath - - - - - - - . to 3. Clockes at 1s: 6d: pr Clocke -	... 7 . 6 ... 4 . 6	paid: Agust: 4.	219.	...12 ...
31.	. mr William Rodger Marchnt his . Mothers ffunneral—Best Mar Cloath . to 15 Clockes at 1s: 6d: pr Clocke -	... 7 . 6 1 . 2 . 6	paid: Agust: 9.	219.	1 . 10 . 0
Agust 2.	. mr Goudy Minister Belliwalter his . Son's ffunnerall pr mr John Cloug'ston . Childers Mar Cloath - - - - - -	... 5 ...	paid: May: 6.	221.	... 5 ...
		16 : 4 . 6			

The prices were subsequently reduced, as appears from the subjoined entry of 5th December, 1716.

1716

Xbr 5. Memorandom this Day Both Session Meet Together & haue Concluded that ye pricess of ye Clockes & Mar Cloathes be as ffolloweth—viz.

Best Mar Cloath in Town	........5.........	in ye Cuntrey	....	10.........
Second Mar Cloath in Town	......3.........	in	Ditto	6.........
Cloath Mar Cloath in Town	......2.........	in	Ditto	4.........
Childers. Mar Cloath in Town	......2.........	in	Ditto	4.........
Childes Mar Cloath in Town	......2.........	in	Ditto	4.........
pr Clocke in ....in Town	......1.........	In	Ditto	2.........

The lost page 1 contained eight entries, relating to the families of Samuel Smith, senr. (10th June, 1712), Carrouth (12th June), Rev. James Kirkpatrick (12th June), James Smith, senr. (18th June), John Shadges (19th June), Colinwood (28th June), John Reed, of the Plantation (7th July), and Orre (9th July).

In the following extracts (taken from page 3 onwards) the name, where no italic letter precedes, is that of the person buried. The italic letter shows what member of the family was buried, whether described as father, mother, brother, husband, wife, son, daughter, child, or grandchild (*c.s* is male child, *c.d* female child, *si* sister) of the person named. A comma has been inserted between the name and trade or place of abode.

1712			
Agust.	3	*w*	James Clark, Laberour
	11	*c*	mr John Shadgs, Marchnt
	21	*w*	John jordgan, Northstreet
Sept	1	*w*	mr Robert Agnew, Mariner
	4	*c.d*	mr Heugh Dayet
	6		mrs Ann Buttle, pr Mr George
	9	*c*	mr Androw Agnew, Couper
Sept	10		David Bucher, Barber
	13		mr ogilbe, Minister in Learn, pr mr John mccMun, Marchnt
	14	*c*	William mccCree, Shew-Maker
	21	*c*	Isaac Monipenny, Beaker
		c	William Liget, Weaver
	22	*b*	mr John young. juner
	29	*c*	mr Hennery Duncan

* These figures refer to the page in the statement of accounts later on.

Octr	11	*c*	Allexdr David'son
	12	*c*	mr Jas Stirling, Malster
	29	*f*	mr Robert Boyde
Nov:	4		George Dunlap, Beaker, Sener
	5		mr Thos orr, Minister in Cumber, pr mr Gilbert Moor, Marchnt
	8	*c*	mr John Kennidy, Cultra
	9	*h*	Widow Mathiss
	13	*w*	Archbald mccMulin
	22	*h*	Widow Spear
	30		Doctr peacock, pr mr Sam: Smith, Sener
Xbr	15	*w*	mr Jas Smith, Sener
	28	*c*	mr John Armstrong, Marchnt
	29		mrs. Elener Hoge, Near Banger, pr mr Hennery Duncan
	30	*c.d*	mr William Dinn, Marchent
1712/3			
Janry:	3	*d*	mr Robert Millikin, Marchnt
	4	*h*	Widow mccIlroy
			James Donnalson
	5	*h*	Widow Alexdr
	11		Edward Nowals, pr mr Sam: Smith, Sener
	12	*m*	mr Ross, at ye Lodge
	16	*h*	Widow Kearnss
	17		Widow Blear
		s	Mr John young, Sener
	19		Elez: Harbison, pr mr Sam: mccClinto
	20		James Realy, Carpinter
	23		mr John Ross, Marchnt
	27	*f*	Heugh Glenhomes
	28	*w*	John Torbourn, Tabacco:
	29	*s*	James Hamilton, in Church-Lean
ffebery.	7	*w*	mr John Smith, Potter
	16	*w*	mr William Willey
		c	mr patterick Kennity
	17		mr Heugh Boyde, Marchnt, pr mr Sam: Smith, Sener
	24	*w*	Thos Clemanss, Carpinter
March	3	*w*	James Homes, Barber
	7	*d*	Widow Carther
	10		mr Heugh White, Banger, pr mr Jas mccClewar, Marchnt
		w	John mccGouan, juner, Milstreet
	13		mrs. White, pr mr Androw Hutcheson
	14		mr John Begly, at Antrim, pr Jas Brown, Sadler
March	20		Doctr Correy, pr Doctr fforguson
	21		mrs. Cambeage, pr mrs. Peacock
1713			
	26	*c*	Richard Whitesid, hatter, Northstreet
Apr	1		Gilbert Marrow, Car-Man, pr mr William Rainey, juner
	21		John Parkhill, pr mr John Armstrong
	25		Capt Richardson, Near Armaugh, pr mr Jno Chambers
	26		Widow Marrow, pr Gaven Marrow
	27	*c.d*	mr Heugh Dayet
May	3		John Chambers, pr Son James
	8		John parker, pr Son John
			Adam Johnston, Milstreet, pr Son George
			Capt Stevenson, pr mr Isaac mccCartiney
	13	*c*	mr Heugh Sharp, Marchnt
		f	James Tood, Carr-Man
	26	-	mrs. Saffage, in New-Toun, pr mr Jno Shadges
	27		Margeratt Rodger
June	3		mr William Johnston, pr mr Thos Bigam
	8		Left William Manson, Near Maheralin, pr mr Jno Chambers, Marchnt
	14		mr Androw Maxwell, Marchnt, pr Son William
	20	*c*	mr John Smith, Marchnt
	21	*m*	Archbald Hunter
	24	*m*	James Tood, Car-man
		c	Androw Johnston, Northstreet
	27	*c*	mr Hennery Duncan, Doctr
	29	*c*	George Prat, Couper
July	6	*w*	Colonneill Mountgomery, pr mr Sam: Smith, Sener
	10	*d*	mr John Black, Marchnt
	12	*h*	Widow Skeets
	23	*h*	Widow Lashley [*Leslie*]
Agust	4	*c.d*	Robert Calinder, shew-Maker
	11		mr Edmond Staford, pr mr Sam: Smith, Sener
Sept	2	*s*	mr Heugh Dayet
	3	*c*	mr Robert Wilson, Marchnt
	6		Hakens mccGill, Esqur — Gill-hall, pr mr Sam: Smith, Sener
	7		James Staford, Long-Cassey [*causeway*], pr Malkam mccBride

Sept. 14 Bealy Addam's, pr mr John Bell, Marchnt
15 mrs. Maxwell, at the Drum, pr mr William Rainey, juner
27 John Cotter, at the-pound, pr mr Michell Greg'ston
Octr. 7 mr Alexdr Hanna at Antrim, pr mr William Hanna
25 John Brown, Tayler, pr mr William Mitchell, Marchent
Nov. 9 mr John Moor, pr mr John Boyde
14 George ffleming, pr Alexdr henderson
12 (*sic*) The Scots Leard, pr David Potter
26 *w* mr Heugh Dayet
Xbr. 7 William Neilson, pr Brother Thos
9 mrs. Addair, at Loughan-More, pr mr Sam: Smith, Sener
10 John mccffarling, pr Thos Neilson
11 Margerat Laughling, pr Jas ffrizell
26 mr ffutt's, at Belliclear, pr mr Brice Blear, Marchnt

1713/4

Janry. 1 mrs Boyde, pr mr ffran Boyde, Marchnt
5 Madam Upton, pr mr Sam: Smith, Sener
13 *h* mrs. mccMinn, pr mr William Craford
15 *c* mr James mccClewer, Marchnt
16 Robert Malkcam, pr mr Robert Millikin, Marchnt
20 mr William Martine, pr Daughter Ann
c mr Sam: Smith, juner
21 mr Androw Hutcheson, pr Wife
23 *d* mr Alexdr Teate, at Cordonall, pr mr Gilbert Moor
24 Cornall John Hamilton, at Laughnavernass, pr mr Brice Blear, Marchnt
ffebery. 19 mr Thos Stewart, at Bellimarrin, pr mr Sam: Smith, Sener
21 mr Thos Winter pr John mccCammon
27 William Murfey, Long-Cassey [*causeway*], pr Wife
March 1 mr Cloud'sley, pr mr Joseph Dabson
7 *m* Margerat Miller
17 Lord Mussrain [*Massarene*], at Antrim, pr mr Sam: Smith, Sener

March 20 *c* mr ffran: Boyde, Marchnt
22 mr Robert Hamilton, at Curdonall, pr son Alexdr
Apr. 3 *s* mr James Smith, Sener
11 *w* mr William Sinkler, Milstreet
Capt James Daben, at Dinnean, pr mr John Black, Marchnt
27 Widow Hogge, pr Thos Arthur, Sener
d John Johnston, Tayler
30 *c* mr James Adair, Mariner
c mr Alexdr Adair, Marchnt
May 1 *c* mr John Armstrong, Marchnt
3 *c* mrs. mccMinn, Widow
w John Pamer, Milstreet, pr mr Jno Heasilton, glover
6 *h* Widow Speaven
8 *c* mr Robert Lennex, Marchnt
9 *d* mr William Sharper, Long-Cassey
10 *s.c* Adam Tonnough, pr mr John mccMunn
13 Thos Tobey, Tidweater [*tidewaiter*], pr John Thomson, juner
14 mr William Hennery, pr mr Robert Millikin, Marchnt
18 *d* mr Edward Wilson
mr John fforguson, poathicarrey
mr Johnston, pr Doctr fforguson
19 *w* George Johnston
20 *c* mr Robert Millikin, Marchnt
mrs. Jean Stevenson, pr mr William Stevenson, Marchnt
21 Widow Bear, pr Androw Logan, Couper
h Widow Dounalson
28 Widow Beggs, pr David Sleater, Weaver
June 1 *c* mr James Adair, Mariner
9 *s* George Lashley [*Leslie*]
15 *c* Edward Riden, Putter
Joseph White, pr mr John homes
16 *m* Alexdr Hamilton, at Cordonnall
28 mr Patterick Isaac, at Beliwalter, pr mr Hennery Duncan
July 4 *c* mr James Adair, Mariner
c mr David mccKnight, Marchnt
5 mr William Shaw, at the Bush, pr mr John Mountgomery, Marchnt
17 *c* mr William Stevenson, Tabacco:

July	17	*c*	mr Michell Menkin
	18	*c*	The Doctr of the Armey
	25		mr Androw Mountgomery, gleaser. pr Wife
Agust	4		Widow Nesmith, pr order of Sessions this Day Meet [*The day was Wednesday.*]
	5		Marrey Grām, pr mr John young juner
Sept.	8	*w*	mr Thos Lyle, Marchnt
	19		mrs. Margerat Euless, pr mr John Blacke, Marchnt
		c	mr John Smith, Marchnt
	26	*w*	John mccffarling
	29		mr Benj: Leggit, Near Carickforguss pr mr Robert Craig
Octr	9		mr Thos Henderson, Tabacco: pr mr John Tayler
	15		David South, pr John All, Loder
	22	*si*	Archbald Hounter, Smith
Nov:	2		mr John Bell, Tabacco: pr mr Jno Smith, Tanner, & mr Hennery Duncan
		w	mr John Tayler, Tabacco:
	3		Widow Loudan, Couper, pr Son Thos Loudan
	4	*c*	mr ffran: Stewart, Mariner
	5	*c*	mr Jas Robison, Marchnt
	23		Marrey fforman, pr Doctr fforguson [*This was a child.*]
	27	*w*	James Tho'mson, pr John Heasilton, glover
	29		mr James mccCappen, Ministr, Belliwalter
Xbr	6		Robert Gib, pr mr Robert Agnew
			mr John Ewing, pr mr ffran: Davenport
	9	*cd*	John Logan, Couper, juner
	13	*w*	Michall Tayler, in Millone
	17		Alexdr Teat, at Curdonall, pr mr James mccClewer, Marchnt
	20		mr Alexdr Stewart, Marchnt, pr Wife
	24		mr James Hamilton, at Cumber pr mr Jno Shadges
	25		mr David Buttle, pr Son George & mr William Cuningham
	27	*w*	Robert Hay, Schooll Master
	30	*c*	mr Heugh Linn
		c	William Sharpley, Tanner

1714/5			
Janry	4	*w*	William mccCree, Shew-Maker
		c	William Sharpley, Tanner
	5	*c*	Thos Eagillson, Weaver, in Cow lean
	12	*s*	Widow Richardson, pr Both Sessions—this Day meet [*The day was Wednesday.*]
	16		Thos Wilson, pr Doctr fforguson
	20	*w*	David fforguson, Sexton
			Widow Gilmor, Plantation, pr Daughter
ffebery	7		mr James mccGee, beyond Holiwood, pr Son Robert
	8		John Stewart, Dunmory, pr mr William Smith, Marchnt
	9	*w*	Androw mccLaughling
		c	mr Robert millikin, Marchnt
		c	mr James Adair, Marriner
		c	Doctr of The Armey
		c	mr Heugh Linn
	15	*d*	Daniell fforguson, Mariner
	21		Widow Sinkler, pr mr David young, Marchnt
March:	15		Marrey Lum, pr Robert Glover
	24		mr John Shaw, pr mr Hennery Shadges
	28		James Bucher, Mariner, pr Robert Thomson, Ship-Carpinter
Apr	3	*c*	Thos Sturgan, Glover
	6		mr Thos Poringer, pr mr Patterick Treall
	8		mrs Margerat Dayet, pr mr John Chambers [*This was a child.*]
	13	*c*	The Doctr of the Armey
	27	*c*	mr John Elsmor, Colectr
	30	*c*	mr Alexdr Stewart, Mariner
			mr John Gaat, Marriner, Bellicloughan, pr mr Robert Androw
			Hennery Carr, Cave-hill, pr brother Jas
May:	1	*c*	mr James Whitelock, Bucher
	2	*c*	Robert Calinder, Shew-Maker
		c	mr Heugh pringell, Marchnt
	19		Madam Duntreath, pr mr William Smith, Marchant
	21		Alexdr King, pr Moses Carr
	25	*w*	Arthur mccKann, pr Son: Sam:
	28	*c*	William Simm, Carpinter

June 15 *c* Cornall Hamilton, [per] mr James mccClewer
Capt Sam: Mountgomery, at Spring-Vaill, pr mr Jno young, Sener
cs Madam Hamilton, pr mr Jas Hamilton, Marchnt
July 11 mr Patterick Shaw, pr mr William Smith, Marchnt
12 mr Thos Stewart, Ballidrean, pr mr George mccCartiney
13 mr Hance ffearly, Near Tonnough-neif [*i.e. Saintfield*], pr mr Jas mccClewer
24 mrs. Lamb, pr John Porter
Agust 11 *c* Patterick fforguson, Mariner
c Thos Eagilson, Weaver
24 *w* mr John mccKnight, juner
26 *c* William Sharpley, Tanner
27 *cd* mr Michall Wood's, at ye Keey
28 mr William Dinn, Marchnt, pr mr Thos Bell
Sept 3 mr David young, pr mr John young
4 mr James Gambell, pr Thos Warnock
5 Mr ffreeland, Minister, pr mr uchtred mccDooll
Thos Scott, pr mrs Ann Martine, at ye Keey
11 *c* mr John young, juner
27 Thos Morton, pr mrs Morton, at Dunmorey [*This was a child.*]
Octr 1 *c* mr Patterick Kennidy, Marchnt
17 John Jorgan, Northstreet, pr David fforguson, Sexton
28 old James Tayler, in Broad Street, Mariner, pr mr Robert Agnew
Nov: 2 *w* James Adair, Shew-maker, pr Jno mccConnall
10 *cd* John Mean, Mariner, pr David fforguson, Sexton
21 Marrey Harbison, pr mr John mccBride
30 Salt John park, pr James parke, Marchnt
Xbr 3 James Adair, Shew-Maker, pr John mccConnall
5 Squr Dabb, pr mr Sam: Smith, sener
15 *c* mr patterick fforguson, ye Cornour [*coroner*]
Xbr 18 mr John Stewart, at Bleariss, pr mr Sam: Smith, sener
27 mr patterick Hamilton, Craig-boy, pr mrs. Coug'ston
29 mrs. Jean Shean, Near-Gleneafey, pr mr Jas Blow

1715/6

Janry 27 *d* Archbald Craig
John Williamson, pr Brother Jas
28 Heugh Liggit, Weaver, pr Wife
ffebery 2 Thos All, Carr-Man, pr Brother Jno
4 Widow Maxwell, Huxter, pr Daughter Margerat
7 *c* mr John Smith, Potter
8 *c* Katherin Scot, Broad street, pr David fforguson, Sexton
11 *w* Robert Maxwell, at ye Keey
13 James Nickels, Barly-Bumper, pr David fforguson, Sexton
14 Widow Mean, plantation, pr Jno Mean, Couper
18 mrs. Orre, pr mr Geo: mccCartiney, Marchnt
19 John Loggan, Couper, sener, pr Robert peagin
20 William Walker, Barber, pr mr James Blow
22 Margerat Eldrage, pr Thos Heaslap, Weaver
25 *c* mr John Johnston, Tayler
28 Joan Ballintine, pr Archbald
James Gillcreass, pr William Garrick
March 18 mr George mccKnight, pr Jno mccKnight, Sener
27 *s* Brice Tayler, horse-jokey
Apr 7 *c* mr Hennery Duncan, Doctr
15 John Stote, pr Son William, ye Couper
28 John Johnston, Barber, at the Keey, pr mr Thos Martine
22 *cs* mr Isaac mccCartiney
23 mrs. Gamble, Petters-hill, pr Thos Warnock
24 *w* mr John Mearss, Minister, in New-town, pr John Thomson in Ditto [*i.e. Newtownards.*]
29 mrs. Kitchen, in Skiginearll, pr mr Robert Wilson

Apr 30 Widow Stote, pr Son William, ye Couper
May. 2 mrs. Joan Hill'ss, pr Joseph Bigers Wife
8 William ffrishell, pr William Blackly
10 Capt Gallant, at Gillgorme, pr mr William Smith, Marchnt
14 *c* William Dunn, King's=Arm'ss
18 Margerat Leass, in Cow=Lean, pr Widow mccKinney, at ye Keey
June. 8 *s* Duncan Lamon, pr Jannet Rain
10 *cs* John Thomson, Mariner, Milstreet
13 James Williamson, pr Jno Mountgomery, Marchnt
John mccfferran, pr Wife
14 *c* Androw Love
James Wattson, pr Son James
15 *c* David Potter
18 John Vent, Sleater, pr Jno Noulty
22 mr Heugh Walliss, in Beliobikin, pr mr John young, sener
23 mr ffran: Shean, Near Gleneafey, pr mr Jas Blow
28 mrs. Walliss, Widow, in Belliobikin, pr mr Jno young, sener
July 1 *c* Widow Scot, pr John Simson
13 mrs. Jean Mushit, pr mr Sam: Smith, sener
w mr William Rainey, sener
14 mr William Craford, pr son David
15 Doctr Alexdr, pr mr Jas Blow
17 mr John Boyde, Mariner
mr Lason, pr mr John Euless, Marchnt
Agust 19 mr Jas Purvess, pr Androw Loggan, Couper
20 mr ffolk White, pr mr William Smith, Marchnt
Sept 24 mr Thos Lowarss, at Donnougha Dee, pr mr Sam: Smith, juner
27 mr Sam: Henderson, Tanner, pr wife
Octr 12 mr James Houd, Minister, Learn, pr mr Jno Mountgomery
25 Widow porter, pr John porter, Couper
Nov. 1 mr Alexdr Adair, Marchnt, pr mr Jas Adair
10 mr mccMulin, pr mr Hadock, Esqur
Xbr 7 Morion Strong, pr John ffiemin, Marchnt
11 *m* mr Haking, pr mr Sam: Smith, Sener
17 James ffife, Chanler, pr Jas Jackson
27 *c* Widow Adair, pr mr Jas Adair
28 *c* mr patterick Kennidy, Marchnt
29 Mr Heugh Moor, at Carrickforgus, pr mr Robert Millikin

1716/7

Janry 9 Major Daben Dinnean, pr mr Gilbert Moor, Marchnt
22 John Hamilton, pr Son Jas
27 mr William Dinn, King's Arm'ss, pr Wife
ffebery 4 James Stirling, Malster pr mr Alexdr Moor
7 mr John Craig, pr Brother Robert
14 *c* mr Robert Lennex, Marchnt
Lord Mount=Alexdr, at Cumber
20 *c* John young, juner
March 4 *c* John porter, Couper
5 John Stevenson, Malster, pr mr John Greeg
8 *c* mr David mccKnight
10 *c* mr William Smith, Marchnt
c mrs. Adair, Widow, pr David fforguson, Sexton
17 *c* William Stot, Couper
27 *c* mr John Smith, Suger
mrs. Mountgomery, at Rosment, pr mr Sam: Smith, Sener
30 *cd* Thos Swendill
gc Nichless Thedford
Apr 2 *c* mr Robert Stewart, Mariner
3 mr John Bell, Marchnt, pr Wife
c mr John Brown, Deary [*dairy*]
11 *c* mr Sam: Smith, Tanner
John Marke, Watter=Carier, pr Jean ffulerton
17 mrs. Roan, at Laughmore, pr mr Sam: Smith, Sener
23 *c* mr Sam: Smith, juner
24 *c* mr Robert Millikin
25 *c* William Sharpley, Tanner
30 *w* Heugh Blackwood, Carpinter
c ffran: Kirkly, Ship=Carpinter
c William Sharply, Tanner
May 9 *c* mr William Woods, at the Mill=watter

May 9 John Martine, at Bearss=Mill, pr Robert Herron
12 *cs* Widow Bell
19 *cs* mr John Johnston, Marchnt
21 *c* mr patterick fforguson, Cornnour
c William ffife
22 *c* David Marrow
c John Johnston, Marchnt
24 *c* John Boyde
28 *c* mr James Blow
c William Boyde, Barber
29 *c* Thos Warnock
June. 1 *c* William Reed, Mariner
2 *c* Robert Donnalson
3 *c* mr Sam: Smith, juner
4 *c* mr William Ringland
John Robb, Mariner, pr David fforguson, Sexton
8 *gc* John Thomson, huxter
9 *c* Robert Craig, Marchnt
10 *c* mr James Blow
c Thos Warnock
13 mr patterick aDair, Minister at Carrickforguss
15 *c* mr Isaac mccCartiney
16 *c* John Reed, Mariner
17 *c* mr John Mear'ss, Minister, New=town
c John Malkam, Tabacco
c mr John Armstrong, Marchnt
July. 2 *c* mr Robert Lennex, Marchnt
8 *d* John Kain, at Carickforgus, pr mr Jas Adair
10 *gc* mr Brice Blear, Marchnt
14 mr Thos Bigam, Merchnt
c mr patterick fforguson, Cornour
c mr Kennidy, of Cultra
17 *c* George Pringell
22 mr John Smith, Tanner
23 *d* David Loggan, Shew=Maker
Agust 5 John mccHallam, at the plantation, pr Thos whiteside
6 *w* mr John Heasilton, Glover
11 Christifor Strong, pr mr Jno ffleming
31 *c* William Stote
Sept 5 Alexdr Smith, pr mr Sam: Smith
John mccKenndery
6 Agnouss Smalchey
8 Alexdr Speaven, pr Robert hunter
9 Androw Loggan, Couper
1

Sept 30 *c* Widow Adair, at Carrick forgus, pr mr James adair
Octr 2 *d* mrs. Ross, pr order of Session
3 Katherin Campble, pr Mother
15 *w* Charless Gordan, Back=ramper
27 Mathow Ronan his Mother in Lawes ffunerall
Nov. 1 mrs. Margerat Gattey, at Learn, pr mr Robert Androw
6 Robert ——Whiteside, pr mr John Heasilton
13 mrs. Rachell Boyde, Widow, pr Daughter Jean
Sam: Henney, penter, pr mr Brice Blear & mr Jno Smith
18 *w* James Guttery, Gabert=Man [*lighter*-man
23 Mr William Rodger, pr mr David Spence
25 mr John Rainey, pr Wife
26 mr Thos Bell, pr mrs. Bell, Widow
Xbr 1 David Sharpley, pr Son William
7 *cs* Widow mccDouall, at the Corn=Mill
14 *s* mrs. Jones, at Mill=Loon, pr mr William Legg

171/8

Jany. 3 George park, Breaser, pr Daughter
7 *w* Heugh Linn
9 *c* Mr Sam: Reed
20 mr Jas park, Marchnt, pr Son Jas
21 *d* mr Geo: mccCartiney
27 *c* ffrancis Boyde
ffebery 2 *m* mr Sam: mccKitterick
7 *c* mr Isaac mccCartiney
8 mrs Boyde, pr mr Sam: Smith, juner
Alexdr Doliway Esqur, pr mr Jas Adair, Marchnt
10 *c* Capt Denty, per mrs. Bealy
gc Widow ffife, pr Robert Jackeson
23 *w* John Clark, Marchnt
25 *w* William Steuard, of Cloghog, pr mr Brice Blear
w John mccCammon
27 William Walliess, at Bely=misca, pr mr Jno Young, Sener
March 3 *c* mr William Mitchell, pr mr Gilbert More
mr John Tomb, Minister, at Mahera=felt, pr mr Joseph Innes

March 4 mrs. Dayet, pr mr Hugh Dayet
12 *w* John patterson, pr David fforguson
17 *c* Robert Deiyeall [*Dalziel*], Carpinter
24 *d* John mccDonnall, Glover, pr mr Jno Heasilton
26 mr Stafey petticrew, Minister in pr mr Brice Blear, M rchnt [*Rev. Stafford Pettigrew, Ballyeaston*].
29 mrs. heterige, Widow, at Marherihall, pr mr Isaac mccCartiney
Left Stevenson, at Killyleah, pr mr Sam: Smith, Sener, Marchnt
Apr 5 William Sharper
11 *w* John Thomson, huxter
15 Widow Hutcheson, pr mrs. mccKnight, juner
23 Jean Bodan, pr mr William Mitchell
25 *c* mr Patt: Kennidy, Marchnt
28 mr John Knox, at pr Son Thos
May 7 Michall Bigger, Smith, pr Wife
June 1 John mccDouall, pr Doctr fforguson, mr Jno mccBride order
9 *w* mr John Brown, Derrey [*dairy*]
12 *w* mr John Chalmbers, Marchnt
15 *c* Mr Sam: Reed
July 1 *w* mr Sam: mccClinto, juner
2 *c* mr John Mathers
c mr John young, juner
c William Colbart, Bucher
c mr Hugh Dayet
c William ffife, Skiper-Lean
w Jas ucher, Back-ramper, pr mr Jas Adair
23 Mr John mccBride
29 Jno mccKnight, juner, pr Wife
c Jas Brown, ye Sadler

[Here begins a new hand, apparently that of William Dick.]

Sept. 3 wdd Loggan, in norstreat
3 *c* Mr. Daniel Musindin, Marchnt
Octr. 10 wdd Davesonn, in the Loang Lean
14 *c* Mr. Donelson, in petersill
16 *c* Mr. Mrsell, the MarChait [*Market*]
Nov. 1 Mr. Stafford, in portglenon, pr Mr. Joseph Innes
2 *s* John mccbide, in Beleygoemarten
3 *c* Mr. Thomas Miller, MarChant
6 *w* Mr. Stnson, in petersill
Nov. 8 Mr. walles, in Celenchey [*Killinchy*] pr. Hugh Walles, MarChant
11 John Johnston, the Tealear
13 Samull Mafet, of bangull
13 *c* David Mcnneight, in petersill
13 John Lusk, Sealor, Living in varen-streat
15 Robert Holmes, in Skepers lean
16 wdd Kirkwood, Living on the Kie
16 Sorgen Finlay, to the Contre [*i.e. some funeral in the country ordered by Surgeon Finlay*]
18 Mr. Muntgomrey, of nutan [*New-townards*]
19 *cs* Macomb mccbrid, in beleyGomartin
21 *c* wdd Anderson, in Millstreat
26 *w* William Hosocke
28 wdd Singelton, in Millstreat
28 *c* Mr. James Adaire, MarChant
Decm. 29 the Revd. Mr. ffillop Meares, in nievtand [*Newtownards*]
29 Mr. Samuell Mccane
30 wdd bell, in broad streat

1719

Janr. 18 *w* Alexander Blear, liveng in norstreat
19 *d* Marey Sorely
30 Annes Muntgomrie, in Church Leain
ffebery 7 John Marten, in the planteshon
9 *m* John Mathies, in the plantteshon
11 *c* Hugh blackwood, Carpenter
13 *c* Allexander Carson
16 *s* old James bigger, the Cotelar
March 1 *c* James Munceye, in varen Streat
21 Majer norie, in poartGonon, pr. Joseph Innes
23 Mr. Boyd, of the Glastry, pr Margret neven
24 *d* Mackom Mccbrid, in beleygomerten
26 Agnes Miller, in the planteshon, pr hir son Alexander
28 *s* wdd Cearnes, bookbinder
29 *c* Mr. James Cobame, in brid eland [*i.e. child of Rev. James Cobham, Broadisland*].
29 *d* William Stevart, in the Loang Casay
Apr. 1 *s* Mr. Dallrumple, MarChant
14 Mr. John MccCallpen, the Taner, in Melstreat
15 *s* Macomb Mccbrid, in belego Marten

Apr. 28 Moses Carr, osler, Samull M^c^Clentons
29 *cd* Mrs. Macerthney, the wdd
29 *c* ffranses Stwart, in Skepers Lean
30 *c* James browne, the Sadler
30 *c* Hugh blackwood, the Carpenter
May 1 Moses Hill
4 *w* Mr. oahtrie M^cc^Doule, MarChant
6 Mrs. Leadeland, pr mr. Will Smith, MarChant
8 *c* Abel Hodskis, nealor
10 *c* Robert Heayes, SColemaster
16 *s* Mrs. Jones, at Milltoon
16 *c* John Mean, in the pantteshon
22 *w* Mr. Hendrie Ealles, sufren [*Henry Ellis*].
27 Mr. John Sanders, in bangul, pr James M^cc^lure
28 *c* Pat fforgeson, at the sin of the son
June 4 John Smith, poater, pr his wife
4 Mr. Robert Agnew
5 Mr. James Muntgomrie, of port Aferey, pr John M^cc^amond
July 2 *w* Mr. walles, in Cekkenchey [*Killinchy*] pr Hugh Wales, MarChant
5 *w* Thomas Qay, in the Church Lean
6 *w* Alexr. Spear, in the Loang lean
7 *c* John beles, in norstret, pr Thomas Martin
9 *c* Mr. James boayd, in learn [*The child appears to have been grown up, and living in Church Lane*]
9 *c* James Moor, in noar streat
17 *c* Mr. Robert Wolson, in broad streat
20 John Shaw, in peterhill, pr Charels Rameg and Gaien Mora
30 *c* Mr. Daniel Musindin
Agust 4 Mr. John Greeg, in norstreat
6 *w* Adam Quaey, Telear
6 *c* Mr. of neall [*O'Neil*] one the Kie
13 weado Clark, in Millstreat, pr hir son
13 Mr. Kill, in Comber parish
17 Mrs. ffeitts, of beleyClear, pr Mr. Wolson, minester [*i.e. Rev. Thomas Wilson, of Ballyclare*].
20 *c* Mr. bankes
26 John M^c^Creath, Carman, in Har= Clus lean
Sept 4 Mr. ffranses Heslip, in Milstreat, Ealseler [*ale-seller*]
Sept 9 *c* William Willey, Caper smith
17 *aunt* Robert Deall
18 John boyd, on the kie, pr his wife
18 Mr. Earter [*Arthur*] Kennedy, of Coltra, pr Alexr Stewart
20 Mr. John wacker, in poartAferey, pr William Stenson
21 *c* Mr. Ringland, gold smith
26 *gc* Thomas Jaslip, Cloath MarChant
27 *s* William Willey, Capersmith
Octr 3 Mr. David Chalmers, MarChant, pr Daniel Musindins
7 *c* Robert Garner, prenter
12 *c* John Shads
15 *s* Mr. John Greer, in Hoalewood
15 *servant* wdd blear
19 Mr. ffranses Ash, in keleaD, pr James bow
26 *d* Edward pearse, Corier, pr Daniel Musind
27 *c* John Suter, Eeal seler, in the Adem and Eave
Novr 1 John m^cc^ffarlien, in the planteshon
1 Samuel Miller, Elseler, in the Egel and Chill [*Eagle and Child*]
2 *c* William boyd, Carman, at the pown
5 Cornl. William Shaw, of the bosh [*Bush*] pr william Smith, MarChant
16 *c* yovng Samull Smith
17 John nowland, his mother, the powlster, pr Mr. Andrew
Decmb 2 Mr. Coalvien, in Dromor, [*i.e. Rev. Alexander Colville, the elder*] pr James M^c^lure
2 Mr. Colena Shaw, of Mahr^e^hoahel, pr Mr. M^c^lure
5 *c* yowng Samuel Smith
9 Mr. James Carr, of Learn, pr James bordges
13 *c* James Snieth, Elde, in nor Streat
16 John Shaw, Esqr., in the bosh, pr Mr. William Smith
23 *w* Daniel ffisher, in the planteshon, pr his Doaghter
24 *c* Thomas lowdan, Couper, in nor-stret

[1720]
Janry 2 *c* Mrs. Garner, A streanger in town, pr Mr. fflimen

Janry 5 *w* Mr. William Jonston, of Celeleah [*Killyleagh*] pr Mr. James M^{c}lure
7 *w* Abel Hadskis, the nealer
18 *gc* Mr. Tatfor, at the Corner
23 *c* Mr. Allexr Chalmors, in peterhill, NarChant
25 *servant* Doct. M^{c}artnay
ffebry 5 *w* Alexander Hamelton, weaver, in Roes Marey lean

[Here begins a new hand, that of Samuel Pentland.]

1719
20
15 *c* Gain Hamelton
19 John Carr, his Mother in Lawe
25 John Loggen, Couper, in Rose mearey Lean
28 *c* Andrew Loves, barberr
Mar 1 Mr. Samull Smith, taner, in norstreat
2 *c* Widd Mathise, in the planteshon
4 Madam Poack, in Coltra
4 *c* Mr. Andrew Agnew, MarChant, in Church lean
5 Gaien Hamelton, Couper, in nor= streat, pr Will Stenson, MarChant
7 Daniel fforgeson, in in norstreat, Mariner, pr his wife
11 *c* Alexander Cilles, Maltmen, liveng in Meistreat
15 w^{dd} Ross, Scoullmistres, in w^{dd} nessmiths Emtrie, pr Mr. Kill-patricket [*i.e.*, *Rev. James Kirkpatrick*]

1720
Mar 26 Andrew Hunter, Cuper, Living in the back of the MarCet House
26 Saruant of Mr. Wales [*Wallace*] MarChent, in neweary, Died in Rowland McGiles
27 *gc* Thomas Haslipe, weaver, in norstreat
30 *c* Joarg Ashmor, Glover, in Milstreat
31 Docter Weare, in Antriam, pr Joseph Innes
Apr 15 oJeam Campel, pr his son John Campel
16 Mrs. ffeearfield, liveng in the County of Down and pariesh of Cell meagen, pr William Walles, Mar= Chent
22 *c* Anntoney Thubrow, Sealowr, in the planteshon
Apr 30 *c* David Kennedy, MarChent, in broad streat
May 2 w^{dd} Knowles, pr Hir Doghter
4 *w* Mr. Jonston, in Reedamon, pr Mr. Arbockels, MarChent
4 *c* Andrew Love, barber
7 w^{dd} Holmes, in scepers lean, pr James Muncey, yonger
8 John M^{cc}rire, tealowr, in roes Mearey lean
8 *c* Mr. William Stenson, MarChant
9 w^{dd} Adaire, in Caregforges, whose boriel was in holewood, pr James Adaire, MarChent
11 Mr. Ritchard Ashmore, pr his wife
12 A jurneymanes of Mr. William Ringland, one the Kie
19 Mr. Hugh Muntgomry, in the Cnoak paries, to his wife
20 James Gutrie, Gabert man [*lighterman*] Living in the planteashon
21 w^{dd} watt, in Jolewood porish, pr hir son James wat, MarChent
27 *c* William walles, tealowr, in mr. Arbockels Entrie
Jun 1 Mrs. Campel, in Antrom, pr Robert Creag, MarChent, in norstreat
3 John Drennan, Ropp macker, pr Samuel M^{cc}Kitrocket
5 *w* Andrew ffiev, in the Long Casae
6 *c* Thom warnocke, in peters hill
7 James Rudeman, in the norstreat
12 James pinkerton, in the loang lean
13 Thomas Gibson, Glower, in Mel-streat
18 Rowland M^{cc}Gill, osler, in Mr. M^{cc}iintons
18 Wdd whitt, on the Kie, pr franses Kirkland
July 1 Wdd Gregg, in HarColes lean, pr Mr. Andrew Agnew, in Church lean
1 Mr. M^{cc}Culoah, in ronels, Esqr., pr Mr. Brise blear
12 Mr. Blackwood, in bangwol, pr David park, MarChent
18 *c* James Warkes, leabrower, in the long lean
20 A sister in Law of James Whotels, in warens stret

Agust 14 Mr. Samull Mcc.Clinton, at the sin of the Crown, pr his son Samull Mcc.Clinton
20 *w* patr Crow, in peterhill
23 Mrs. Catraien balief, in the new boldings, pr Mr. James Martien, in Lesburn
27 patricket brown, in peterhill, pr his brother, John brown
29 wdd brumfild, in scepers lean, pr hir neas, Elisebth Thomb
29 wdd Harper, in broahshan, pr Mrs. Harper, MarChant, in broadstreat
Octr 12 *d* Edward Mccleaney, in the ffalles
22 *c* John Cunigham, in the milfeld lean
26 Wdd Simson, MarC, per hir son William
27 *c* John Jonston, MarChent
29 Mr. Joseph Chochren, MarChent, to his wife pr. Samull MalCom, Tobaco Spener [*spinner*]
Novmbr 1 Robert peagon, at the Corn mill, pr his son Robert peagon, beacker
15 Wdd ffinlay, pr William paterson, in norstreat, showmacker
18 Mr. Loang, MarChent, in Mahrihoohel, pr Mr. James Mcclure, MarChent
Desmb 1 Mr. Eatten Euwat, Minester in the parish of Cloagh milles in the County of Antrim, pr Docter Mcc.neall
1 *c* Thomas Miller, MarChent, at the Stonbridg
15 Andew Mcc.kie, truper, pr his wife, the stamper
15 *c* John Stockman, Sealear, pr his wife
19 William Grriear, in Holewood, pr his brother
30 *d* John Cille, in the Loang Casea, pr his brother Samull Cille
c Edwar whittlocke, Marchent

[1721]
[Jan] 6 A step Doghter of Robert Crofords, on the Kie, Maroner

1720
Janr 9 *s* Macom Mccbride, in belegomartien
9 *c* Mr. William Muntgomry, MarChent, in norstret

Janr 14 Mrs. balentine, in Millstreat
17 *c* David Kennedy, MarChent, in broad streat
21 *c* Allexr. Henderson, Gleasowr, in norstreat
21 John woodes, at the fowr Lone Ends, melone, pr Joseph innes, MarChent
31 David Stoormie, in belegomarten, pr William Stenson
31 *w* John Gelston, in Cnoack parish, pr James Hamelton, in Caselreah

1720
1
ffebr 3 *c* Samull Gillmor, in the loang Casea

[Here begins another hand, apparently that of Andrew Agnew.]

h Wid Callinder
wid English
mr. Jno. Smith for Hugh Wallace
Tho: Lawry
Wm. Rainey, for Arthur Maxwell, Esq.
c David Murray
c Ed: Whytelock, some time before

1720
1
febry 17 Jno Semple
18 *w* Jno martin
25 Wid: Creg, Clonavy
mar: 2 *w* Jas. Smith
7 Wm. Whytler
12 Wm. Martin
13 *c* mr. Joanes
14 James Connyhy (?)
23 *c* mrs. Loe
24 *w* Jno. Barre
25 *c* mr. negam (?)

1721
apr 5 Wid mcc.William, by Jean Willson
12 St John Johnstone
16 Janet Demster
18 *d* David Logan
20 Jno mc.Glochlin
c Richd. fferralls
25 mcc.Kennay, widow
27 *c* Wm. ffife
may 3 James Boyd
Agnes Hethington
7 Adam Quae
16 *d* Jno mitchell

[Here begins another hand.]

1721			
Jun	12		Mr. Cunnigham Esqr., in the Count of Dearey at Springhill, pr Mr. Samull Smith, MarChent, yownger
	12		Thomas blayen, Eallselar, in noarstreat, pr his wife
	13		Jean wolson, in Churck lean, pr John Charters
	29		Mr. Hamelton, that was Cast Away on the Dock, pr Robert hamelton, MarChent
	30		widdo brown, in the falles
July	1	*c*	William Roper
	7	*d*	John ffisher, sawer, in the loang leain
	8	*c*	Docter Doncan, potegar
	12	*w*	William Simson, seaDler, in norstreat
	21	*s*	James Cowter, in the Loang Casae
	22		william Simson, the sadler, pr John Ros, David morrey
	26	*c*	John Stowart, living At the browrie [*brewery*]
Agest	4	*d*	Mr. Mcmurlian, living in Dene Goar [*Donegore*]
	5	*w*	ArCheabel Mintgonry, taner, in noarstreat, pr Mr. Hamelton, in Holewod
	9	*c*	Hugh backwood, Carpenter
	11	*c*	Hugh Qaey, Teallowr
	12		William Mcrea, Showmaker, pr John poarter, Coper
	18	*c*	John Smith, MarChant, in broadstreat
	19	*c*	yowng Charels Ramage, in peterhill
	29	*w*	Hugh Muntgonre, in Dinygor, who Died in petterhill and was boried in Shankel, pr his son Robert Muntgomrie
Sept	3	*c*	John Gregg, the Smith, in norstreat
	3	*c*	John Clotrdy, botcher, liveng at the Melgeat [*Millgate*]
	8	*w*	Mr. Robert Hamelton, pr brown Joarg M'Cartnay
	14	*c*	Mr. William gowane, in peter Hill
	18	*c*	Mr. Joarg Gutrie, MarChent, in broad streat
	24	*c*	Mr. ffearol, in peterlill
	27	*c*	Pat Kennedy, the MarChent
Octr	3		Mr. Killoe, in the Cumber pearish in the Cownty of Down
	9	*c*	Mr. warnock, in peter hill
	17	*b*	Robert McGee, in Holewod, pr Robert McGee, in waren streat
	17	*c*	Mr. Joannes, Exise Man
	18	*w*	Edward pearss, the Correr [*currier*] in nor Streat, pr Mr. Lille
	24	*w*	John Scoat, in the ffalles
	30		John Sharpe, the Smith, pr Mr. Sharpe, the MarChant
Nobr	5	*c*	John McGown, in Melstreat
	8		Madom paotenger, in Careforgous, pr Capt Jmes Maxneel hamelton, in the Drum
	9	*c*	Robert tamson, Sealer, liveng in Melstreat
	9		John Suoters, Elseler, pr his wife
	10	*c*	Mr. John fforgeson, potegar
	12		John bowman, the Meason, pr his wife
	10		the Colectors leady, pr Oabedia Groaves
	16	*c*	John MccLonehan, in norstreat
	17	*c*	Mr. Robert Hamelton
	22		David Staford, in the ffalles, pr his brother Alexr
	22	*c*	Mr. Middelton, Eall seler, in norstreat
	23	*c*	James Muncie, in scepers lean
Desm	2	*c*	David Kenedye, in broad streat
	8	*w*	ffransess Malcom, peterhil
	11		William Arther, in norstreat
	21	*c*	David potter, in town
	30		James Stafor, at the fforth River, pr his brothe Alexr
[1722]			
Janr	2	*s*	the Revd Mr. Mcckraken, in lesburn, pr Mr. Cornel brise
	3		Mr. Orr [*Rev. Thomas Orr*], in Combar, pr his Clark
	3	*c*	Thomas Qua, in Church lean
	6	*c*	Joarg Ashmor, in melstreat
	10	*c*	Mrs. Smith, in the Shogerhovs, pr hir son John
	11		Mr. briss blear, pr John fforgeson
	26		Thoomas Stowart, prentise to Mr. Arbockesl, pr yowng Samull Smith

Janr 27 wdd Gregg, pr Mr. Willson [*Rev. Thomas Wilson*] Menester in belley Clear
27 *c* Mr. James Adair
27 *c* John MccGown, living at the Melgeat
28 William Gaieit, Living in beley Esten, pr Samull Smith, Siner
30 *c* William Carsan, in Mellstreat

1721
22
ffebr 6 *c* Mr. Ree, Ship Carpenter, in waren streat
8 Mrs. McGill, in lurgan
9 Mrs. Ashmot, in Mill Streat, pr hir Son John Ashmor
23 Mr. Mathis, weater on the Kie, pr obedia Groaves
23 Mr. Talford, pr obedia groaves
Mar 10 *c* Mr. Hugh Lin
10 *c* John stoakman, Marioner, pr his wife
14 Capt whitside, living in Mellone, pr his wife
16 *s* the Revd mr. Mccapien [*Rev. James M'Alpine*] Minester in beleynehinch, pr William Stenscon, At the Ston bridge
20 *c* John Daben, Liveng in peter hill
21 *s* Thamas warnock, in peter hill
21 widde Campbel, in melstreat, pr Mr. Craford, Minester [*Rev. Andrew Crawford, of Carnmoney*]
22 Samuel Mcckitterick, in norstreat, pr his wife
29 David Kennedy's brother, taner, in norstreat
29 A brother of Archelb Miler, ffidler, living in noarstreat, pr Martha ward
30 *c* James Moor, Sealler, in warean streat
31 *c* David Spence
Epr 1 *c* John Goarden, MarChant
1 *d* Robert Sinkler, in the loang lean
2 *c* Hugh Linn
3 *d* wdd ffisher, in Casel streat, pr hir son
5 old Mr. Innes, pr his son, Mr Joseph Innes
6 *c* Thomas whitsid, Ship Carpenter, on the Kiee

Epr 8 *c* Mr. Eddmeston, pr Mr. James Adair
8 John Haselton, Elder, pr his wife
9 *c* Capt MccColoah
10 A saruant of Mr. blow, prenter
12 Mr. bankes, pr Mr. ObeDia Groaves
14 *c* Staford Millford, Tealowar
17 Henery Poater, barber, in in mill streat, pr David Poater
26 *c* Mr. John Clark, MarChant
27 Mr. William Roadgers, Potegar, pr David Spence
28 *c* Pat fforgson, at the fowr Corners
May 2 Mrs. Clamens, pr Docter Donkan
6 *c* Joarg Rosbrogh
9 olld Mr. Reanney
10 *c* John Mcamon
12 *c* Gorge Ashmor, Glouer, pr John Ashmor
14 *c* Docter Donckan
(*sic*) 91 *s* Robt MccGee, in waren Streat, who was boried in holewood
26 *gc* brown Gorge McCartnay
28 *c* Hugh Pringel, MarChent
30 *s* wdd Campbel [*three cloaks apiece were ordered by* the Capt of the tealoars, the Capt of the beackears, *and* the Capt of the Show-mackers]
31 Mr Hendrey Donean, to the ffunerall of his Mother in law
Jun 3 *c* Docter Doncam
4 Mr. David spence, MarChent, pr his wif
4 *c* James Dicke, Miller, of the Mallt mill
7 John browns Mother in Law, Chanelar, in Mellstreat
9 Leard Hamelton, Living at Holewod, pr James MccLure, MarChent
9 *c* James Mafert (?), the beacker
13 *c* James Grear, Shoemacker, pr Mrs. Agnes, botcher
16 *c* Antoney Conegham, sealler, living at the browrie
21 *w* John Hathorn, Cornmill
26 *w* Mr. Mccquearn, in beley Manoh [*Ballymena*], pr Alexr moar, peterhill
July 3 Robt Adams, Ship Carptenar, pr James Wear, Mariner

July 9 Mr. Baniam Patterson, MarChant, pr his wife

11 brise blairs wdd paid 12 shilings that she had in her hand for the Revd Mr. Cowters [*Coulter*] Doghters funerall

12 *c* Andrew Skellin

13 brown Gorge McCartnay, pr his son George

14 *w* Will Arter, pr willam Stoatt, Copar

16 *w* Mr. Teatt, potegar, in Lesburn

17 *c* John Maxwel, hoxter, norstreat

21 wdd Cawall, in hallewood, pr Mr. MccClure

Agst 5 *c* wdd MccGill, Elseler

6 Mr. Robert Andrew, MarChant, pr his son Gebrall

8 Mrs. Ann Martin, pr Mr. ffransess Joy (son in law)

11 John ffreaser, in beley Gomarten, pr John brown his Stepson

11 Samull beggs, Showmacker, Long lean

17 *c* Mr. Ardbockel

17 Robt Hamelton, Copear, one the Kie, pr his wife

29 Mr. Black, Combar, pr Doctr Donckan

Sept 15 Mrs. Maxwel, pr Patricket Maxwell, who Died in beley Manoh and was boried

17 *c* yowng James Smith, malltman, in norstreat

20 Mr. John Kennedy, of Coltra, pr yowng Saml Smith

24 James Iralland, in tempell patricket, pr his Son John Iralland, in the fall

Oct 7 *w* George Roasbrogh

14 *w* James brown, SeaDler, in norstreat

23 *s* Alexr Moor, peterhill

23 wdd Deaveson, warenstreat

24 *c* Mr. Danield Mussenden, MarChant

25 James Creaghton, Ropwack [*rope-walk*]

30 *c* borbra McGill, hole of the wall

Novr 3 widd McCadam, longcasa

3 Mr. Edward Whitloack, MarChant

15 James McTear, MarChant, pr his brother Sam Mctear

Novr 18 Mrs. Sharp, fowr Corners

18 *c* Hugh Pringel

27 Neall boy Mcneall, who Died in Doctr Mcnealls, pr EarChabld [*Archibald*]

30 Mrs. Gallant, Gelgoram [*Glengorm*] pr ArChebl Mcneall, potegar

Desm 11 Mary Millen, melstreat, pr David Kennedy, taner

22 *c* Mr. boyd, of the Gleasrie [*glasshouse*], pr Mrs. Marget Neven

22 *w* James layon, Ship Carpenter, plantesion

27 *c* Mr. John Johnson, MarChent

27 will Anderson, Eall selear, in broad streat, pr Mr. James blow

1723

Jan 7 *c* Robart Haye, Scolmaster

10 Mrs. Lee, in learn, Pr Joseph Innes

11 David Park, pr his brother James Park

12 *c* Antoney Coke, Sealer, Roas Marey lean

19 ball Jean

20 *d* Temothy ffulertan, Stronmilles

24 Margrat Cambel, Long lean, pr Thomas Mconall, Shomaker, norstreat

28 *c* John Clark, MarChent

28 *c* Robart Hamelton, Hoxtor, Norstreat

1722
3

29 *c* Robt Hay, Scolmaster, Market house

ffab 3 Dauid beggs, Carman

6 *c* Mr. Pat Smith

7 *c* Clamens McCadam, peterhill

12 *w* Hallbert Carr, in peterhill

13 *c* Robart Dalzel, Carpenter

16 *c* will walless

17 *s* Thomas bornsid, whelwright

24 wdd MallCom, pr wrs blear, broad streat

27 Archabld Creagg, pr his wife

Mar 8 Thomas Arther, Norstreat, pr will Stoat, Copar

14 Hanna Jolmbes [*Holmes ?*], hoxter, in norstret, pr brother James Holmes, wiggmaker

16 Mrs. Neall, Kerkdonall, pr hir son ArChebld Neall

Mar 23 Captr Treall, pr Joseph Podgenar
24 Mr. Edward Whitsid, Melone, pr his son John whitsid
Apr 3 Mrs. Andrew, pr hir Son Gebrall Andrew
3 *w* Daniel ffisher, pr him Selfe
7 *w* Sam Mckelvey
12 *c* John Johnston, MarChent
18 Neclous Sharp, preanties with Mr. will Mitihel, MarChent, Pr his brother John Sharp
21 *c* Thomas Mclune, Glover
24 *w* Joohn Anderson
28 *c* william Lason
29 John beard, Loang Casa, Smith

1723
May 13 Richard Lamb, pr John poarter, Couper
13 wido Johnston, Waller, pr John brown, Chanler, Melstreat
13 Mr. Gordan, bandbridg, pr John Gordan, MarChent in town
13 A Scoatch Man that Dayed in town
19 Alexr Mcmun, pr Mr. John Mcmun, MarChant
22 *c* John Alld, Cloath MarChent
23 *si* William Colbart
24 *c* Joseph mines, Sealler, Potengers Entrie
James Carithers, Glover
31 *c* John Geades, Carier, Norstreat
Jun 2 *w* David Kennedy, MarChent, broad Streat
3 *c* will Maxwel, MarChent
5 *w* Mr. Roase, Lodge
10 *w* Sam boman, gleaser
16 *c* Doctar Duncan
16 *c* James white, Copar, Roos Marey lean
18 *d* wdd Cearns, pr hir mother
21 Margrat Robeson, Scepers lean, pr hir Sister, widdo Mclelan
22 *si* Squear Dason, Dasonds bridge, Pr Joseph Innes.
July 3 *c* John brown, Norstreat, Meallman
8 *w* William Combe, at millwater
11 *d* wdd boyd, glesrie, pr Margrat Neven
16 *w* Mr. Dickson, Cerkdonel, Pr franses boyd, ChurChlean
July 17 *c* John McDowal, heresons lean
17 *c* william McConoah, tealowar
20 Joseph barklow, Carpenter, Pr his wife
27 Robert McGeies Mother, who was boried in holewod
29 *c* John McDowall, Carrman
Agest 3 Thomas Miller, MarChent, pr Pat forgeson
5 John Means, Sceper, planteson
6 *c* John McDowall, Carman, Harklovs lean
6 *s* Mr. McCen, helsborow, pr EAdam McCen, prentis Mr. Ecels (?)
Mr. Shavegg [*Savage, per*] Mr. Sam Smith, junr
9 Agnes Hunter, Church lean, pr Hilley Hunter [*her brother*] Retrney [*attorney*]
18 wdd Hogsid, pr hir Doghter Reachel
21 *w* Mr. Neagen, pr obedia Groave
26 *c* John McCart, taner, peterhill
31 Mr. William MuntGomry, pr his wife
Sept 9 *c* Mr. Dunlap, living in Mr. Andrews house
9 *w* Mr. Stoward Esqr., Celey mon [*Killy-moon*], pr yowng Sam Smeth
24 *c* Sam McClontow
Octr 1 *w* James wright, Tealloar
2 *c* Mr. John wallas, MarCent, broad streat
9 *c* David Dunn, Mariner, in scepers lean
20 william Simes Mother in Law, Carpenter
28 olld Doctor fforgeson, pr Capt McColoah
29 *c* John Mcgown
31 Mrs. McGlahlen
31 A sarvant of Mr. Maxwels of feney broag
Novb 2 ffransis boyd, Church lean, pr his wife
5 Mr. Carr, in belymanoh, pr Mr. wason, broad streat
9 *c* Mr. will Leg, in Mellon
11 Thomas Allan, at the brurie, pr Patrick Smith, browrie
13 wdd McDowal, back Ramper, pr hir Doghter Agnes
17 *c* Isaac Ramag, peterhill

K

Novb 24 Mr. Stell, banger, Pr Mr. James McClure
26 *c* Allexr Deaueson, Chanlor, in ChurCh lean
27 Jonathan Moor
28 *c* nathaniel Moarison, ChurCh lean
Desm 1 *c* Mr. James Adair, MarChent
8 Mr. John yowng, MarChant
5 *c* William Greage, Teallor
11 A Child who was A frind of Madam Dabes, pr Madam Dabes [*Dobbs*]
12 *s* baniam McDowall, Dunegor, pr Mr. McLure
14 John Sherp, in hoolowod, Pr Mr. Rowland Sharp
21 *c* Jorg Carsan, waterman
22 wdd Thamson, pr Mr. Ramse
24 *c* Mr. John fforgeson, potegr
24 *c* Mr. Joarg McCartnay
25 warham Smith, Church lean, pr oabida Groaves

[1724]
Janr 4 Long Margrie, pr Mr. James blow
10 *w* Hugh blackwoo, Carpenter
17 *c* Cornall fforgeson
17 A streang [*stranger*] in town
21 *s* John fforgeson, potegar
27 *w* Robt Lawe
ffebr 2 John Shaw, Shoger howse, pr Mr. Jon Smith

1723
4

4 *c* Mr. will Mitchel, yownger, MarChant
5 the Leat Sr John Roding [*Rawdon*], in Mayorah [*Moira*], pr Mr. MccCartney
6 Samull Holmbs, broad streat, pr his mother
8 *c* John Gregg, Smith, in Norstreat
11 John Campbel, Lodger in Mr. John Mcmuns, pr Mr. James burges
13 Thomas Eagelsom, weavor
13 *b* Mr. John Clark
13 *d* Willm Hasock, melfild
14 *c* James Moor, Miller, ffall mill
17 *d* Jon McGown, Mill streat.
18 Richard farels Mother in law, living in tempelpatricket
24 *c* Mr. John Smith, Living at the sluse bridge

ffebr 24 *s* Mr. Colam, Returney
28 the Leatt Revd Mr. Sam getty in learn, pr Mr. gebrall Andreow
Mar 2 *m* Mr. John Clarke, the MarChent
4 wdd watt, pr Mr. John Hamelton, beleynefy
7 *w* Thomas warnock, peterhill
7 *w* John Ashmor, Glower, Melstreat
8 the Leat Revd Mr. Williamson, in belenhinch, Pr William Ringland
9 Mr. umfres, pr Mr. John Holmbes
15 *c* John Ashmor, Glover, Mellgeat
17 *c* Alexr McKown, Carman
31 wdd fultan, Millfeilld Lean, pr John Holmbs
31 *c* Jno Eggers, Smith, Rosemerylean
Epr 1 *c* william Delap, Last maker
4 Joarg boyd, in John Demster, pr Doctr McCartney
6 *c* Capt McColoh
10 *c* David Craghton, Seallor
15 *c* the Revd Mr. Harper [*Rev. Samuel Harpur, of Moira*]
24 *c* Mr. John Colman
30 Willilliam Thamson, Seallor, plant-eson

1724
May 5 William McGlathrie, in the Lang Casa, Pr Jon Cunigham
5 *m* Mr. Jon Stel, potgr, DonoGhiede [*Donagheady*]
13 *w* Mr. Townsend, Mellgeat
15 Mrs. Cobam, in Hoolewod, pr Mr. Jon Smith, MrChent, broad streat
16 *c* Will Ringland, Gold Smith
17 *c* Andrew McComb, Millstreat
18 *c* James Thomason, sealler, Milstreat
20 *w* William stoat, Copar, norstreat
Jun 2 *s* widd Cearns
s Samull Gillmor, Long Casa
7 *c* Mr. will Maxwl, MarChent
13 *w* James Hamelton, peter hill
14 *c* John Eruen [*Irvine*], Millfieldlean
15 *si* Mr. James Cobam, Jolewood, Pr Mr. Jon Smith
24 *c* James Hamelton, Marinor, Pr Mr. James Hameton, at the bredg End
28 *w* Mr. Jon Gorden, MarChant
July 1 *c* Robt Dalezel, Carpentar

July	6		David Kennedy, North geat
	8	*c*	Mr. William Maxull, MarChent
	12		Mr. Jon Mcmun, MarChent
	12	*c*	Will Teatte, Glover, Millstreat
	13	*c*	Mr. William Townsend
	15		Sam Carnohen, Long Casa
	19	*c*	Jon Sttel, potger
	21	*c*	Joseph Coahren, MarChent, at the stonbridg
	29		Joarg Ashmor, Hatter, in Mill streat
	30	*w*	Mr. Oakes, in Glean Eauey, Pr William Sinkler, in Melstreat
Agst	8	*c*	Mr. William Reany
	8	*c*	James Dicke, Miler, in the Malt mill
	9	*c*	Angos wacker, on the Kee
	14		Dauid Kennedy, broad streatt, pr Jon Rose, potegar
	15	*c*	Mr. Hugh pringel, MarChent
	18	*c*	Mr. Mathies, in the ffalles
	19		Will Tood, Carpenter
	20		A saruent of Mr. Innes
	22		Mr. Porter, in Kirk Donall, pr Mr. Andrew Agneow
	23	*d*	Mr. Mathies, in the ffalles
	26	*c*	Mr. James Park, MarChent
	26	*c*	Mr. William Raney, MarChent
	27		William Mcreight, Glouer, Mills streat, pr Alexr Kille
	28	*c*	Mr. Jon Horgeson, potegr
	30	*w*	yowng Samull Smith, MarChent
Sept	8	*c*	Sam Mclento
	8	*c*	Richard Cowter
	13	*c*	Jon stowart, browrie
	13	*c*	the Reud Mr. fflatchard
	14	*c*	Abell Haskeson, nealer
	20		Mr. David black, Pr his father Mr. Jon black, fowr Corners
	28	*c*	Mr. pat Kennedy, MarChent
	30	*c*	Mr. Henderson, Clark to Mr. McCuloahs
Octr	7	*c*	Mr. Daniel Mosentin
	8	*c*	Edwar Harie, botche
	11		Mr. Donelson, Gleneauey, Pr Mrs. Campbel, beacker
	11	*c*	Mr. Adam Gutrie, MarChent
	14	*w*	Alexr Craford, at the Maltmill
	16	*w*	Samull Marttien, in Hoolewod parish
	18	*c*	Jon Glean, in the hole of the wall
Octr	20		Mrs. Glespie, att nuttan [*Newtownards*], Pr Mr. Edward Whittloack, MarChent
	22	*c*	Mr. William Mittcheal, MarChant, at the stton bridge
	23	*c*	Mr boall, seallor, warenstreat, pr Mr Rea, seallor
	25	*c*	Mr Cobam, Retorney
	28	*c*	wdd miller, at the Sttonbridg
	28	*c*	Robt boall, in broad street
	29		Mrs Eruen, Comber, who was boried in this town
	30	*c*	Widdo Miller, Sttonbridg
	31	*c*	Mr William Mittchel, MarChent, att the Stonbridg
Nour	1		old Mr Tattford, pr Mr Arther Tattfor
	3	*c*	Mr Robert boall, broad streat
	8	*c*	John Lawes, norstreat
	9	*d*	Andrew Derumpel, MarChent
	12		Mr Alexr Storvard, pr Mr William Ranie, MarChent
	12	*s*	Jon Garner, beacker, in Rosemary lean
	14	*c*	Mr Jon Walles, MarChant, broad streat
	23	*c*	Jon Sheain, in Gleneauey
Desm	1		Mr Agnew, of Celwaghter near Learn, pr Mr James burges, MarClent
	2	*m*	James Holmes, weauer, in Rosemery lean, pr Edward Loggan, Carman
	4		James whitt, Copar, in Ross mary Lean, pr Mr Anttney Harentton
	5	*c*	Mr Robert Creag, MarChent
	6	*c*	Mr Rusell, living in mellon, pr mr william tomsend
	8		Mr Jon Porter, Copar, Pr Mr Andrew Agnew
	16	*w*	Mr Andrew Delrumpl
	22	*c*	David Mcneight, in peterhill
	24		Mrs Moor, who was Jonethon Moors widow, Pr hir son Jon moor
	29		Mrs Gresell Reney, Pr Mr Jon Ecels
	30	*c*	Mr James Adair, MarChent
[1725]			
Janr	2	*c*	Mr James Mairs, Living in broad streat
	4	*c*	Mr Sam McLento

Janr 9 *w* Hugh uanse, Labrer, Living in Rosemery lean
10 *c* Jon brow, in peter hill
13 *gc* James Law, Hoxter
15 Isack Ramige, Carman, Pr Charels Rainge
28 *c* Jon Hana, Chanler, living in Norstreat
29 John Mcarttnay, Gabert man, Living in the plantesion
31 *c* Mr Robert McCapon, living at the Mill geat
31 *c* Mr Richard ffarell, living peter hill
ffebr 6 the Leat Squeair Hatreckt, Pr Mr Isaac MccCartnay
8 Samull boyd, Meall man, in Church lean, Pr Hugh Smith, in Church lean
11 *f* Mr Capt Maxwell
17 Mrs Petterson, MarChent, at the Market House, Pr Jon Johston, MarChent
18 *s* Mr James Hamelton, bridgeend
19 *c* Hugh Marteen, Pr John Thomson
20 Mr. Cromie, High Shieref, Pr Mr Jon Smith, Marchent, Juner
21 *w* Thamas Marten, Market House
22 *c* Mr Hugh Pringel, MarChent
25 wdd McComeby, back Ramper [*Back Rampart*]
26 *c* Adam Patey, planteson
Mar 5 Mr Mcanse Kirkland, shipCarpner, living one the Kie
11 *c* Mr Cobam, Returney
12 James brown, in the ffales
12 *c* Edward whitloack, Mar Chent
15/14 Mr Jaremy Campbell, who was Loast in Garmoyle, pr his son
17 Euphams Rush, liuing in Rose mery Lean
17 *c* Mr William worthenton, living in Church lean
18 Mr Casky, who was lost in Gar moyle
19 *w* Mr Russel, in Hoolewod
24 *m* olld Sam Smith, living in Dunegoar, Pr Mr Pat Smith
30 Arther Kell, in Holewood, pr Mr James MccClure

Mar 31 *w* William Anderson, living At the salt water bridge
31 Mr Roper, sealler, his Mother in law
Epr 2 *c* Jon Glen, hole of the wall
3 *c* Mr Cobam, Retorney
4 *c* Alexr Daueson, Selear
5 John M'Dowall, Carman, to his wife
8 olld John Adames, Norstreat
9 *c* Thomas ffeare, living in the Rosemary Lane, Marinor
10 *c* David Leathem, Gon Smith
13 Andrew McCone, Carman, Longlean, Pr Jon Ecles
15 *c* William yeward, tobackow Spener, in milstreat
21 *w* Antney Thobron, seaman
21 *c* Jon Chapman, Marinor, living in potengers Entrie
24 *c* Mr Jon Johnston, Marchent
May 15 *c* Jon Starlen, in the ffalls
19 *c* Jon Starlen, in the ffalls
19 *c* William bearrd, Marinor, living in the plantesion, Pr Mr Jon Carr, Elder
26 William Sallter, Living in the ffalls
26 *c* Mr Jon Stoakman, Marinor
28 *c* William Amblem, Coper, at the browrie
Jun 8 Jon neckelson, in the Long lean, baggman
16 *w* Mr Hugh Pringel, MarChant
18 *c* william Smith, Shogarhouse
22 Mr Hugh Cunigham, Clark to the old Mitinghouse
23 *c* Mr McClure, MarChent
29 Mrs Maxwel, of Obeday Groaues, of ffiney broag
30 Robert Skery, kie porter
July 1 Joarg Jhnston, Barber, in Mill streat
9 *c* Mr Jon McCartney, MarChent
13 *c* John Patterson, barber
19 Mr Greansheals, Carmoney
20 *c* William Geall, Shomacker, noarstreat
23 Mr McCologh, in Ronaldstown, Pr James McClure

Agest 6 *w* Mr Jon Johnton, in Norstreat, beacker
15 Mr John Challmbrs, MarChent, Pr his Son James
Sept 2 old Mathew Garner, Pr Mr Arther Tattford
3 *c* Sam Smith, Junr, who was boried in holiwood
5 *c* Mr Edr burt, sufron in town [*Benn gives the name as Nathaniel Byrtt; he died in office*].
14 *c* Jon Smith, son to olld Samull Smith
18 *c* Samull Smith, Ealle Selar, ffowr Corners
27 John Comack, in Mayrogh [*Moira*], Pr Mr John Jhnston
Ocbr 6 Robert Calhond, beacker, Pr John Rose
13 Mathew Garners wedo, Pr Mr Arter Tattford
13 Mr William Smith, Pr his brother Mr John Smith, Shogerhouse
Novb 8 Mr William Raney, MarChant
16 Cesie [*Keziah*] Tonough, back Ramper
18 *c* Mr Archbald Mcneal, potegar
28 *c* Robart Thomson, ship Carpenter, plantesion
6 wdd Granger, Mill streat, Pr hir son in Law James Thonson
7 *c* William Hamelton, Cooper, in peter hill
13 Mr John Grrefen, Comber, Pr Mr Antoney Harenton
20 Robart Cauer, in Celead
25 *c* william Lason, smith, Church Lean
1725/6
Janry 5 *c* Thomas M'Clune, Glouer, in Rosemary Lean
12 John Ree, ship Carpener, living in waren streat
12 *c* Caluen Darlen, at the Sluse bridge
21 Patricket withers, Copper, in warenstreat, Pr Mr Andrew Agnew
25 *c* william McCologh, Telear
28 *c* Mr ffrases Cromie, MarChent
Febr 14 *c* Cornall Edward brise, who was boried in Balleycarey

Febr 18 *s* mrs Ross, at the ston bridge, Pr hir son John
MarCh 7 Cristian Poag, Living in Rosse marey Lean, Pr Mr Thomas Storgan
9 Mr Edward Willson, in waren streat
11 Archbald Moor, marioner, Living in waren Streat, Pr his wife
18 A Leftenanen of the man of war that is at Learn, Pr Mr James MccClure
29 *c* Mr William Staford, Marioner, in Clogstans Entrie
Aprl 2 *m* William brown, at the fforth River
7 Mr Antony Harenton, Rosemery lean
13 *w* John Brown, in peterhill
15 James Mcartnay, Sufron in Town, Pr his brother Jon McCartnay
15 *c* Mr John Smith, Son to olld Samull Smith
15 *c* John Hall, Coppar, in Scepar Lean
17 Mr Jno black, Pr Mr James Arbockels
May 5 John Stwart, in Mellstreat, who was saruant to Mr Kelpatricket
7 *w* Mr Jon Sharp, MarChent, in broaD streat
7 *c* Jon fframe, weauor
8 *c* Edward Loggan, burnCarier
10 Mrs Arther, at the fowr Corners, Pr hir Granson, Arther Burt
27 *d* Mr Isaack Mcartnay, MarChant, on the Hanower Kee
30 *c* Mr William Walles, MarChent
Jun 14 *c* James Willson, butcher, in Rosemery lean
15 Alexander Hotcheson, at the millewater
15 *s* John Irwen, wever, in Jorges Lean
19 *c* James Weear, Marioner, at the ffott of Potengers Entrie
23 *c* Mr Maxwel, of ffeney Broag, Pr Corn Brise in Town
23 *b* Mrs Clogstan
27 *c* Docter Delap, at the Ston bridge
29 *w* Mr Woodside, Marioner, at the ffot of waren Streat

July 2 Daniel ffisher, Mariner, Living at the Kee, Pr his wife
4 c Moses Hill, butcher
8 c Robt Henderson, in beleninch, Pr Alexander Henderson, Gleser
14 d Mr ArChbld Stowart, in Comber
22 m Mr Samull McTearr, in norstreat
Agest 1 c Dauid morrow, Teloyr, livng in broad streat
2 c margret Ruebery, in the Long Lean
5 c Dauid Layons, in the Long lean
11 w Robart McCapen, Taner, mel geat
16 w Dauid Morrw, Teallowe, waren streat
20 olld Mr James Smith, Pr his son James, norStreat
29 Mr Joseph Innes, Ston MarChant
Sept 1 olld Mrs yowng, Pr hir Son Hugh yowng
8 c Mr James Monsie, in Scepars Lean
10 2c Thomas Lowrie, beacker
13 c Capt James McCologh, in Waren Streat
26 c Mr James Moncie, in Scepers Lean
8br 11 c John yowng, Carppenter, living at the now Erexon Geat [*New Erection, i.e. Third Meeting-house, gate*]
15 c Mr James Moncie, in Scepers lean
27 c Mr Adam McCen, in waren Streat
29 c Alexr Henderson, Glesor, in norstreat
Nor 2 c Mr John Ald, MarChant, in the back of the MarCethouse
3 c Mr Robert McCapen, Taner, mill-geat
4 c Thomas McConel, Shoe maker, in norstreat
17 c will McDowaille, ffidler,
18 c David Pinkerton, beacker, in the Ston bridg
20 c Mr Willian Maxwell, MarChent, one the Hanouer Kie
29 c Mr John Seadg, one the Hanouer Kee
Desm 7 c Mr william Mettchall, Elder of the olld metting hous
8 Mr John Hamelton, beleny fey
10 f Ritchard Skerie

Desm 11 c william McCologh, Tayloar
11 c Samull mettchall, in noarstreat
13 c Robt Dallzel, Carpentar
27 c John boel, in harkels lean, weauer
31 s Mr John walles, at Doaggh, Pr mr John walles, in broad Streat
31 Mr James Smith, in Noar Streat, Pr his wife

[1727]

Jner 8 c Mr Sam McClenton, uentnar
10 c Samull willson, Stashenor, son in law to wdd Cairns
13 Mr MComb, in Doagh, Pr Mr John walles, in broad Streat
22 Mr John Eacles, MarChant, in broad streat
30 Mrs Grrean, in waren streat, Pr Mr Patrect Kennedy
ffebr 5 Henrie Jones, Pr his Sone Thomas, in Peter hill
6 c Robert Creage, Pr John walles, in broadstreat
15 John ffllemen, beyont the Long bridge, Pr his wife
3 Mrs becerStaf, Pr Mr John Smeth, at the Sine of the Pecok
4 c Mr Arther Telford
5 c Mr William Walles, at the bredg End
19 c Patreck Kenneday, MarChent
19 c Mr John fforgeson, Potegar
19 c Mr James yowng, MarChent
20 Mr David McCnaight, Peter Hell, Pr his wife
25 Thomas Mcneight, Teallor, Leiuing in Rosse marey Lean, Pr David Morrow
29 Mr Dickson, in Comber, Pr John Colbert
31 c Ritchard ofarel, in Peter Hill
Apr 1 Jean Marten, in ChurCh Lean
10 d Hugh Sharpp, in Kirk Doneall
13 d Mrs Manken, in veran streat
13 d John Gades, Corier
17 gc Allexr Moor, in Peter Hill
17 c William wyly, Coper Smith
(*sic*) 12 c wdd Smith, in nor Streat
27 c Mr ffranses Cromie, MarChent
May 2 s ArChbld Stwart, in Comber parish

May	6	*c*	David Pinkerton, Living at the Ston bridg
	9	*c*	John Mcfferan, Living in Rossemarey Lean, tealower
	15		Mrs Mirifeld in Lisburn, Pr Mr Thomas Lill, MarChent
	20		Mr Andrew Dalrumpel, MarChent, Pr Mr James Dallrumpl
	20	*c*	Mr James Parkes, marChent, at the Ston bridg
	20	*s*	Parson Hamelton, in banger, Pr Mr Sam Smith, junr, MarChent
	20		Sara Mcneall, planteson
Jun	3		John McDowall, Pr James mcDowll, in Holewood
	3	*c*	Mr Jon Moor, Scoll master
	10	*c*	John umfres, Scollmaster, in waren Streat
	11	*c*	Mr John Allde, MarChent, in Potengers Entrie
	25	*c*	mr John Macartney, MarChent
	29	*w*	Thomas ffeare, in Rose Marey Lean
July	11	*c*	Jorg brakenrig, Gleaser, in Rossemarey Lean
	15		Mr Ritchard Ashmor, hatter, in mell Streat
	16	*c*	Jorg brakenrige, Gleaser, in Rosse Morey lean
	17	*m*	John Irland
Agest	9	*s*	John hamelton, Living in neow Combe
	10	*c*	mr Robert mcCapen, taner, in Mell Streat
	24	*c*	Mr John Johnson, MerChent
	24	*c*	mr James begger, marChent
	26	*c*	widdo Smith, in norstreat
	26	*c*	ArChbld mcneall
	28	*c*	mr James bigger
Sept	1	*w*	williamson, in Caselreah
	5	*c*	Jorg Guttrie, MarChent
	11	*c*	George Gutrie
	11		mrs Clugston, Pr hir son the sofren
Octr	6	*c*	mr Sam Mclento
	7	*w*	James barnet, in melstreat
	8		Dauid morra, Taylor, in waren Streat, Pr his wife
	25		mr William Arbucklé, Pr his father mr James Arbuckle
Nor	5	*c*	william Sinkler, in melstreat
	6		Mrs Jean Clugson, Pr hir brother the Soueran in town
	17	*m*	Mr Cobam, Returnie, in Town
Desm	5		John boall, marinor, in waran Streat
	14		A Streanger, living in Jorg Stevens Entrie, mell Streat, Pr Madam Dabb
	23	*c*	John willson, in Rose marey Lean, weauer
	26	*c*	Thomas wason, Carpeiter, in Rose Marey lean
	27	*c*	William Staford, marioner, in Clogsons Entrie
	28		Robert Coper, in Hugh Pringels
[1728] Janr	18		Mr Harper, Living in Glanarm, Pr mr Samull Allen
1727/8 ffebr	3		A Streanger that Dayed in the ffar End of ChurCh lean, Pr mr Joseph bigger
	5	*b*	Alexr orr
	21		Mrs Donelson, Pr Hir Son in Law mr James McClure, MarChent
Mar	6		olld Mrs Ewens, in Peter Hill, Pr mr Jon Armstrong
	12	*c*	Allexand Henderson, Gleasor
	14		A frind of Mr James blow, A yowng woman who Dayed in his House
	15	*c*	John bowall, weauer, in Harklos Lean
	15		John fforgeson, son to olld Docter fforgeson, who dayed besides Dogh, Pr mr John forgeson, Potegar
	21		Robert Morra, Taylor, in Rose mary Lean, Pr his wife
	23	*c*	mr wear, maironer, in the fut of Potengers Entrie
	29	*c*	Alexr Henderson, Gleasor, in norstreat
	30		olld mrs Todd, Pr mr Thomas Lille & mr John Smith, in broad Streat
Aprl	4		olld william mclelan, in the Long lean, Pr mr mcDowalld and mr Robert mcGee, in Scepers lean
	5	*w*	Thomas Agnewe, scleater

Aprl	6	*c*	William mcCologh, Taylor
	7		John Read, Labror, in the Plante-shen
	8		mrs Innes, Pr Mr Joseph Innes
	9	*c*	John McDowall, Carman, in Peter hill
	11		mrs Comock, in Myroah parish, Pr mr John Smith, at the Pecoak
	15		olld James Orr, in Comber at the Dam, Pr Allexr Orr, marChent
	17	*w*	Hugh Kennedy, in the Longlean
	19	*w*	William mcLelan, in the Longlean, Pr mr oahtrie mcDowall and mr Robert McGee
	23	*d*	Mr James Moor, in the ffall Mill
May	1	*c*	William Moor, Chanler, at the Sluse bridg
	2	*c*	mr Jno Sttell, Potegar
	6	*c*	Jon Stell, Potegr
	6	*c*	william Endslie, Glower, in Rosse mery lean
	7	*c*	william Hanna, Taylowr, in Church lean
	14	*d*	mrs Camel, beacker
	17		Mr John Clark, MarChent, at the Market House, Pr his wife
	17		John Jakes mother in Law, Show make
	28		James Thamson, Marioner, living in melstreat, Pr his wife
Jun	3	*c*	Thomas mcConell, showmaker, in Norstreat
July	8	*c*	mr William mittchel, MarChant, Living besids mr John mcCartnays
	12	*w*	mr William ffarlie, at Lisburn, Living in Lesnetronk, Pr mr James mcClure, marClant
	15		David Pinkerton, beaker
	19	*c*	mr Gillbart mcDowall, MarChent
	19	*w*	mr Wallter Cromel, Pr mr James mcClure
	20		Chancler Mcneall, of Port of ffery, Pr mr James McClure, marChant
	28		mr John Kinkaid, Pr mr James McClure
	30		mr Allexr Moor, Marchent, in Peter Hill, Pr mr Getty
Agest	15	*c*	Allexr Henderson, Gleaser
	17	*gc*	John Johnston, beacker, in nor-streat

Agest	25	*c*	Jorge Johnston, barber, in Mill Streat
Sept	9	*c*	mr Hugh Linn, Living in Casel-streat
	20		olld Madam Dalaway, Pr mr Samull Smith, MarChent
	24	*c*	mr James Henderson, Living in warensteat
	26		mr John Taylor and his mother in Law
Octbr	7		Mrs bruse, Pr mr John Roose, MarChent, at the Stonbridg
	24	*c*	Thomas Lowrie, beacker.
nor	5		Jorg williamson, Smith, in Church lean
	6		mrs Hutcheson, near beleclair, Pr mr John fforgeson, Potegar
	23	*c*	william Osborn
	28	*c*	mr Andrew Smith, marChent
Desm	1		Gillbart moor, Sinr, his mother in Lawe
	13	*c*	James Campbel, watterman
	18	*gc*	James Lawe
	27	*w*	mr Robt Johnston, in mellone
	29		mr Thomas Lyle, Pr mr mosentine
1728/9			
Janr	4		mr John McCartnay, marClent, Pr the Reud mr Samull Helleday
	6	*s*	Andrew barnet, Pr mr John Smith, marChent, broad Streat
	15		mr John Shaw, beleytwedy, Pr mr James mcClure
	18		Capt McCologh, in Ronaldstoun, Pr mr James mcClure, marClent
	20	*c*	mr John Sharpe, MarChent, in broadstreat
	27		Mr Walles Granmother, marChent in broadstreat
ffebr	5		widdo mcCanlie, Pr mrs mcCanlie, liveng in the plantesion
	9		margrat miller, in mr David Cra-fords, his seruant
	10		mr Samull McClenton, Pr his wife
	13		A strenge, Pr mr Jon Smeth, in broad streat
Mar	2		mr John Smith, Liung in Mr Pa-tricket Smiths, MarChent
	9	*m*	Ringen [*Ninian*] ffresel, in Long lean

Mar 20 *w* Georg Campsie, in norstreat
24 Gaien Hamelton, Pr mr Jon Colbert
Epr 1 *c* mr John Johnston, MarChent
2 *w* Doacter Smith, in town
8 *c* James Singelton, in mill ffeld lean
13 *c* William hamelton, Cooper, in Roose mereylean
23 *c* mr John Mairs, in Town
24 *w* william mathies, in Loonglean
30 *m* Thomas Lowrie, beaker
May 1 Iserall Coates, Liung in the ffalles, Pr obedia Groaues
3 Thomas ffeares, Sealler, his mother in Lawe
7 mr John mcCeben, at Kerkdonel, Pr mr Adam mcCeben, marChent in town
20 the Reud mr John Mallcom, in Dun morey, Pr mr John walles in broad Streat
20 *c* Mrs Petecrow, in NorStreat
Jun 13 *c* Robert Ashmor, Hatter
13 *c* Alexr Daueson, Marioner
16 Daniel Handerson, tobacones, Pr mr Robert Henderson, Taner, in norstret
16 *c* mr Samull Mittchel, MarChent, in norStreat
July 8 *c* A sister of mr Samull Mitchell, in norStreat, MarChent
14 *c* william Henderson, taner, in norSt
20 Mr Adams, yearn Marchent, At the Ston bridg, Pr his wife
25 *c* mr William Sharply, Taner, in norstreat
Agest 4 *c* David Layens, Cafey Hous
5 *c* mr william Staford, Marinor
13 Agnes Leas, Pr Ronold, in Mr James blowes
14 Mrs Leas, Pr hir Son Ronold, in Mr James blowes
20 Andrew Tood, in the Countie of Down
22 mr James Woods, Living at the ffowr Lone Ends in mellone, Pr his Doghter Mrs mccGee, in warenstreat, weddo
26 *c* John Dreanen, Roper, in NorStreat
L

Agest 29 Olld Madam Pottenger, Pr hir Son mr Joseph Pottenger
Sept 1 *c* mr ffranses Atcheson, Eall seler
4 *c* mr James Henderson, Living at the Shoger house
5 *c* mr John walles, MarChent, broad Streat
7 *c* mr William mcCaulie, liung in the plant teshen, sealer
10 *w* Andrew wattson, Carman
11 *c* James nelson, Carman, tor Streat
14 *c* Samull brown, Peter hill
20 wido mcCalester, in the Long lean
22 Mr John Sharp, in broad streat, his onkels Doghter
22 *c* Andrew mcComb
Octr 3 *c* mr William Mittchel, MarChent
8 *c* Dauid Craghton, Marinor, in Norstreat
11 John fram, weaver, Peter hill
11 *c* Rittchard Offerall, Petterhill
14 *c* John osborn, beaker, in melstreat
15 *c* Geiorg Carson, water man, at the plantteson
20 *c* John Slloan, beacker, in norstreat
Nor 3 *c* John mcDowald, Carman, in nor-Streat
5 *d* wildow Parkhill, in Peter hill
10 *gc* John Gades, at north Geat
23 *c* John Taylor, tobackenst, in norstreat
25 *c* widdo boyd, in mr Allexr yowngs howse, tenenenenan
Dems 1 *c* John mcmorey, Taylor
2 *c* william moor, Chanelar, at the sllus bridg
7 Gain Rodgers, in Long lean, Pr his ffather william Rodgers
13 olld mrs Craford, Pr hir son Dauid Craford
16 mrs Sinkler, Pr mr Dainel mosentine
16 John osborn, beaker, Pr his wife
25 Hanna bell, Pr mr John Collman, Clark of the olld meting house
25 Olld william Rusel, olld Park, Pr his Son Georg Rusel

1729/30
Janr 13 *c* mr James Challmbrs in waren Streat
21 John brown, in Peter hill, Pr John Singelton, weauer

Janr	23	wido Maxwel, norStreat, Pr David Craghon, Marinon
	30 *c*	william Innes, whipmaker
ffebr	4	A stranger in the Contre, Pr Alexr orr, marChent
	4 *c*	Thomas Geleland
	7 *c*	Mr Sam Smith marChent
	12 *c*	Isaack AGnew, Copper
	24	the Revd mr James bruse, Keleleah, Pr mr John Smeth, at the Peoack
	24 *c*	mr John Knoox Gold smeth
Mar	4	John Catterwood
	4 *c*	John Mcquesten
	16 *c*	John umfres, Scoll master
	24	Mr Matthew Ramsey, Clark of the neow meting house
	28	Mrs Read, in Kellenchie, Pr mr James McClure
	30 *c*	James Loaggan, Eall seler, in norstreat
Apr	8 *c*	John mcGlahlen, brower
	11	Nathan Smith, Pr John Hughs, in Carmoney
	18 *c*	mr James ballief, Marioner, Pr mr Hoadkis, nealer
	19 *c*	Moses Cunigham
	24 *c*	Georg Gemeson, beacker, at the Ston bridg
May	1	Thomas Agnew, Pr his Son in Law, mihel mcfeall, butcher
	13	wido mcCormick, in the Long Lean
	16 *c*	mr Cobbam, Returnie
	18	John Marten, Long lean
	27	oll mrs Rittchie, Pr hir son Robt Dallzel, Carpenter
	30 *c*	Thomas ffife, Carpenter, in norstreat
July	4 *c*	mr James bigger, marChent
	18	Dauid Potter, Church lean
	19 *c*	mr John Gordon
	20 *c*	John Picken, in Long lean
Agest	17 *c*	John mean, Shomaker
Sept	12 *c*	James baillef, Marinor
	22	Mrs Ashmor, Hatter, Pr hir Son Robert
Octr	4	brown Georg mcCartney wido, Pr mr Patr Smith, MarChent
	30	A brothers Child of Walter Sandelens
	31 *w*	Rittchard ffinnley, Town Sargen

Nor	10	Madan shaw, in Lisburn
	14 *c*	mr Daniel Mosentine
	17	mr Georg Manken, at the millwater
	21	Thomas Marten, in Rose marie Lean, Pr his ffather in Law Robert Mcffeall
	30 *w*	James monsie, in Long lean
Desm	1	mrs Rosse Hamelton, Living in mount Hamelton, Pr mr James mcClure, MarChent in Town
[1731]		
Janr	2	Allexr orr, for his Cosens ffunerall
	3 *w*	Mr Arther Tattford, Pr the Revd mr Neclous Tatford
	7	the Reud mr Sinklear, Pr mr John fforgson, Potegar
ffebr	15	Olld widdo boyd, in the Plantesion, Pr mr William McCanlies, maioner
	27	mr William mcwhorter, in Carmoney, Pr mr Joseph Jinnes, MarChent
	28 *c*	mr William Mcuckelwreth, marChent
Mar	7	mr John Damster, Pr his wife
	19	Doacter Cromie, Pr his brother in Law Mr John magenis, Liung besids Drummor
	19	mrs fforgeson, in tampel Patreck parish, Pr mr Jon Smith, in broad Streat
	27	mrs Manken, at the Millwater, Pr hir Son Thomas manken
	28	mr oferall, in Peterhill, Pr his wife
	30 *c*	widd bell
Apr	9	mrs Hadenton, in Town, midwife, Pr mr Joseph Innes, MarChent
	27	mr James Robeson, marChent, in Norstreat, Pr his wife
may	27 *c*	John Eger, Smith, Rose mery lean
	31 *c*	Astrenger, in the Long lean
Jun	4 *si*	mr Adam Adam mcCeben, marChent
	9	mr James wear, maironer, his mother in Law
	10	James Scoat, in Drumbo
	18	mrs Johnes, play howse
July	8 *s*	mr Georg maCertney Esqr
	13 *c*	James Rodgers
	15	John Donelson, in Church Lean, beacker

July 15 neas of Toallen, in the ffalles
22 *c* John mcCert
24 *c* Thomas willson, barber, one the keay
Agest ye 3 Maigor blaire, Livng at Carn Castel, Pr mr James burges, marChent
12 William Geals, Showmaker
12 Robert ffisher, in the ffalles
27 Astreanger
30 *w* Mr wear, one the Kee
31 Robert Scoat, taylor
Octr 17 *s* mr Robert Donaldson, in Peter hill
18 *w* Thomas Gilleland, buttcher
Nor 2 David Throw, miller, of the Corn mill, Pr his wife
3 *d* widdo Agnew, at Cewaghter [*Kilwaughter*] Pr mr James burges, marChent
6 John Gaddas, Coriner, Pr his wife
15 A frind of mr Joseph Innes, in the Contre
15 olld mrs Tavernor, in the ffalles, Pr Sam McCadam, in the Long Casa
15 *c* Sam Joy, meason, in norstreat
20 *w* Thomas Singlton, in the Long Lean
24 *c* mr ffranses Cromie, MarChent
29 wido ffife, Pr William mcCullogh, Taylor
Desm 6 Mr ffranses Cromie, Pr mr James bllow
6 Capt Hamelton, Living in Cushin-Dun, Pr mr James McClure, marchent in town

[1732]

Janr 6 *c* John ffife, Sope boyler, in Norstreat
7 Mr Patrick Kennedy, Marchent
9 *c* Thomas Gueleland, butcher
9 *c* Samull mcCalliue, Museshenar
10 *c* mr John Maiers, in town
22 *m* Lahlen Mcneal, mairnor, in the planteshon
25 A sister in Law of Thomas Gilleland, botcher, in Town
ffebr 1 *c* mr John Alld, marchant, in Town in the back of the Grean
Mar 2 mrs black, at Drummor, Pr mr mosentine
Mar 16 *w* mr John Mairs, in town
16 mr Hugh Sharp, Pr mr John Sharp
Apr 2 mrs Joanes, in melone
7 mr James Hamelton, Chaneler, Pr mr James McClure, in town
7 *c* mr Hugh Linn
21 *c* will Cros
May 20 wido bell, at the Coaue hill
21 Astrangers Chill, Pr James Easdealld, botten maker, in Town
22 mrs bleair, living at CarnCasel, Pr mr James borges, marChent, in town
Jun 2 *c* James Lure
3 *c* mr Robt Ashmor, Hater
19 *c* John Jake, Showmaker
23 william Dicks mother in law
24 *c* James Rodgers, ship Carpenter
July 5 Alexr mcDowalld
15 *c* mr John Ashmor, marClent
20 *d* David mcmen, at the Coawe hill
Agest 3 *c* will Lason, Smith
7 Maigor upton, in tampelpatrek, Pr mr James mcClure, marClent, in Town
8 *s* the Reved mr wolson, in beley Clair, Pr mr James burges, in town
15 *w* John mcClune, mairnor, Pr his brother Robert mcClune
22 *s* Pall Redd, in Tampelpatrek, Pr John Sempel in Norstreat
Sept 2 *c* Thomas whittsid, Ship Carpenter, one the kee
13 widdo Craford, one the kee, Pr John mcCeben, Copper
Octr 1 *c* Thomas whittsid, one on the Kee, ship carpenter
15 *c* Hendrie fegen
16 *w* Robert mcfeall
21 necloas Sharp, Pr his sisters
23 *w* William osborn, butcher
nor ye 17 *c* mr Patr Smith, marChent
ye 16 mr Gabriel Andrews, MarChent, Pr his brother Hugh Andrews
ye 26 James boyds mother in Law, marinor, in scepers Lean
30 mr John Taylor, in broad streat, Pr his wife

Dems 7 *w* Andrew mcClenchie, Dunmorey
10 *w* Timothy Shelds, beaker, in Rose mary lean
10 *s* John Taylor, Carman
14 John Kerns, snuf man, Pr his mother, wido Kerns
19 William Lowrie, buttcher, Liuing at the wattersid, Pr his wife
21 mrs Shaw, of beley Gelly, Pr mr James McClure, MarChent
22 *s* the Reud mr Clugston, in Larn
24 *c* Antoney Thobron, sealler
25 mrs Potter, mother in Law to Robart Armstrong, marChent in town, whos mother in Law Liued in Kelenchie
27 wido swondeall, in HarColes Lean, Pr hir Doghter marey and Thomas Lowrie, beaker

[1733]

Janr 15 mr James Challmbrs, marioner
16 *c* John Gafoge, botcher
22 Robart Ranton, Pr mr Robart Donelson
27 *c* mr James yowng
31 *c* Georg Ross, ship Carpenter, in the backplantesion

ffebr 16 *w* James Layon
17 *c* mr Isaac Agnew, Copar
19 mr Gelbart Moor, MarChent, Pr his Doghter Elisabeth
20 Peter Alexande, in Peterhill
21 *c* Robt Stwart, in Drumbo, Pr Robert mckee, in the Paresh of Drumbo, in beley Coaen townland
24 *c* mr Isaack Agnew, Copper
24 widdo Guning, in Roess merie Lean, Pr mr ffranses Atesion, at the Punshbowl
25 mrs Creag, harclos Lean, Pr John Henderson, weauer
26 *w* John ffife, barber, Pr hir son John, Chanler

Mar 3 *w* Mr John Sharp, MarChant
5 mrs mcCullogh at Shaes bridg, Pr mr Dauid Craford, in Town
16 William Scoat, in Drumbo, Pr neuin mckee, in belecoan
17 *c* Georg Johnston, melstreat

Mar 18 william ffergeson, at the Clownie, Pr his son Georg ffergeson
20 *w* mathew mcnealley, Pr John Sempel, Peter hill
26 Harcoles mcGomrie, Esqr, in beley Leson, Drumbo, Pr Capt Hamelton, Drumbeg
26 *c* mr Hugh yowng, marChent
27 wido Sttwart, Plantesion, Pr hir son in law, Antoney Thobron, marioner

Apr 3 *w* William ffergson, in the Clownie,
24 Pr hir Son Georg ffergson with Sqr mcartney Colector
22 *c* mr William Walles, at the bredg End
24 Hugh Morrow, in the ffalles
28 *c* John Orr, in Drumbo

May 9 *c* mr William Sinkler, in mellstreat
12 *c* mr James Caallmbrs, marinor, in waren streat
13 olld John mcfaden, Pr his son Hendrey mcfaden, barber, in Church lean
19 mr William Henderson, for two children at Deferant times
20 *c* mr John Jack Show maker
20 *c* John forsieth, Taner, in Ropwack
24 *c* William Kenen, Ship Carppenter, in the Plantesio
27 *c* Georg Lashel, Cardmaker
31 Georg Swarbreck, liuing in the ffalls, Pr his wife

Jun 2 *d* James Smith, Coppar, in Roesmary lean
2 *c* mr Hugh Pringel, marChant
3 *c* John Dowald, bangbeger
3 *c* John fife, Sopboyler
4 *c* Robert forsieth, in the falles
4 *c* wido Arbockels, in Rosse marey Lean, Pr olld mrs Ardbockels
6 *c* Samull Mittcheall, in norstreat
6 *c* mr Paterek Smith, marChant
9 *c* mr Robart walles, marChant
10 *c* mr Isaak Agnew, Copper
10 mr Joseph Innes nephew
12 Hendrie mcGomrie, Carman
12 *c* John boald, weauer, in Rossmerey Lean

Jun	12	c	John mcGlahlen, hoxter, in norstreat
	14	c	Charles Garner Gardner, Marinor, at ye Slows bridg.
	15	c	John Lawes, Hoxter, in norstreat
	16	c	James Sowrbot, on the kee
	17	c	James mcCalserar, in norstreat, Carman
	18	c	James nelson, in norstreat
	19	c	Charles Garner, Marinor, at the Slows bredg
	21	c	mr William Mittchall, one the hanouer kee, marChant
	23	c	Willm Lason, smith, in Church Lean
	24	c	William Hamelton, Copper, in harcoles lean
	24	c	Thomas Anderson, opeset [*opposite*] to mr Archbld mcneall, Doctor
	24	c	John Gafogen, botcher, in melstreat
	25	c	Georg Endsly, in norstreat, Glower
	26	c	William mathies, Carpenter, in the Long Lean
		c	Patr mackrorey, marinor
	29	c	samull brown, Peterhill
	29	c	mr James Moor, marinor
	30	c	mr James mcClure, MarChant
July	1	c	Robart mcClelan, in skeprs lean, Marinor
	1		neuen Parker, in ye Long casa, Pr John Sempel, in Peter hill
	3	c	Dauid Teatt, Leuing one the hanower kee
	4	c	John fflemen, in Long Lean
	6	gc	Robert mcfealle, in Ross merey Lean
	9	c	James Perey, weauer, in Harcoles lean
	10	c	Thomas Wason, Carpenter, in Ross merey Lean
	10	c	Mr William McCanlie, Marinor, in Plantesion
	12	c	mr Handley, heall maker, in warenstreatt
	15	c	William hanna, Taylor, in Church lean
	15	c	James boyd, in skepers Lean, marinor
	15	c	Adam Patty, Plantesion, marinor
July	15	c	Widdo mcCartney, Plantesion
	16		John Wollson, on the kee, Pr his wife, Ene keper
	18	c	mr John Johnston, MarChent, in Town
	18	c	William Nutt, hatter, in Church Lean
	19	c	Georg Carsan, waterman, in Plantesion
	19	c	John Mean, Marinor, on ye olld kee, Pr his onkel, Alexr Tamson, waterman
	19	c	Robert Dallzel, Carpenter
	19	c	John wharton, Church Lean, Showmaker
	20	c	William Hanna, Taylor, in Church lean
	21	c	John McDowald, Carman, Peterhill
	21	c	Wido Swarbridg, in ye ffalls, Pr mr James Moor, in ye ffalls, Elder
	22	c	Patreack harbert, Carpenter, in ye Plantesion
	24		Robert Gastowns Mother, who Lived at ye 4 Corners and was boried at Antrem, Pr hir Son Robert Gasken
	27	c	James McClune, butcher, in Town
	28		olld William fferguson, at ye Clownie Pr his son Georg with ye Colecter
	31	c	John Winentown, book binder
Agst ye	1	c	John Mcfaden, hatter, in Church Leat
	3	c	Rittchard ffenely, Surgen
	9		Elinor McCrom, hoxter, Pr William Lason, Smith
	10		mary McDowald, Pr hir brother
	20	c	John Teatt, Glower
Sept	6	c	Samull brown, Peter hill
	16	c	Widdo Donelson, in ChurCh Lean
	17		olld widdo Arbockels, Pr mr James Arbockels wife
	24		mrs Mash, Pr hir son mr Hugh Pring, marChant
Octr	3	c	William PateyCrow, Taylor
	15	c	Hugh barneat, who was boried in sant feield
	20		Wido McCotchen, in Plontesion
	23	2c	the Reud mr Mihel bruse
	30		Dinis ohegan

nor	6		mr William Sttenson, at bears bridg, Pr mr John Knox, Gold-smith, in Towin
	11	*m*	mr John Ross, marchant, at the stonbridg
	17	*c*	Patr Agnew, marinor
	18		William Anderson, at the whitt hovse
	25	*c*	Andrew Harper, taner, in norstret
Desm	3	*c*	mr Hugh Linn, melstret
	7	*w*	Dauid Loggan, in Rossmery Lean
	9	*c*	Hugh barnet, in Town
	9		Alexr besbbe, at ye Long -Casa, Pr his son John busbe
	15		William Ashfield, in ye falls
	23		Widdo McDowald, at ye brurie
[1734]			
Janr	3	*w*	William Lason, in Church Leam
	9	*m*	William Kennen, Ship Carpenter, in Cow Lean, near the Plantesion
	10		mrs Potter, Pr mr Robert Arm-strong, marChent
	17		mr Andrew Kelsay, in at the Rogh-forth, in Tampelpatreck Peresh
	22		mr James Park, marChant, in Town, Pr his brother, Arthur Park
1733/4			
ffebr	4		mr oahtrie mcDowald, Pr mr John Holmbs and James burdges
	9	*c*	William brown, in beleygomarten
	10		wido mcCormeck, Pr mr Samull Willson, Prenter, at the Stton bredg
	16		mr Hugh yowng, MarChant, at the ston bridge, Pr his brother mr Allexr yowng
	19		William mcClenchy, in the falles
	21		oll widdo mcClelan, in scepers lean, Pr mr John Chapman, marinor, in warenstreat
	22	*c*	mr James mcClure, marChant
	27	*c*	Robert Thamson, Marinor, in Mill-stret
Mar	8	*w*	James Singeltow, weaver, in Melfel Lean
	14	*c*	William Sttaford, Marioner, in Clugstons Entrie
Apr	5		mr Aunger Robeson, Eall seler, Pr his ffather, John Holmbs, at ye Adam & Eve
	8	*w*	Mr John Carr, at the olld Park
	14		Arther Graye, shoger man with mr Pringel
	18		Widd Robeson, Longlean, Pr hir son John Robeson, Copper
	21	*c*	Alexr Mogerland, butcher
	26		James McGee, at ye fowr Lonends up melon, Pr his son Thomas
May	2		ye Revd mr [*William*] Taylor, in Carn Castel
	2	*c*	John Wharton, show maker in Church Lean
	8		Mr David Craford, in Town, Pr Mr Archbald mcneall, Doctor
	25	*c*	Samull Ratliue, waterman
Jun	5	*d*	Widd mcCall, liuing in Dunmory
	7	*c*	John Kean, Living in melon
	12	*c*	James yownge
	23	*c*	Widd fferall, in Peterhil
	30	*c*	mr Archabld, at the fowr Corners
July	1	*c*	Robert Lowrie, Carpenter
	3	*m*	Mr Hendrie mcCulogh, in Ronolds-town, Pr mr mcClure
	8	*c*	mr Craford, in Tempelpatrek Peresh, Pr William brown in Peter Hill
	12	*c*	James McGefort, botenmaker, in norstreat
	13	*c*	John Picken, Carppenter, in the Longlean
	16	*c*	Robart Ashmor, Hatter
	18	*w*	Alexr McCelie
	22	*c*	Andrew Sloan, Taylor, Church lean
	23	*c*	Dauid mcneight, book binder
	24		mrs boggs, Astrenger
	29	*m*	mr Alexr Sttaford
	30	*s*	John mcfferan, Taylor
Agst	3		Doacter mcneall, Pr mr Archbald mcneall
	7		mr whittfeald, shoger man, Pr mr benjam Gegg and Compnie
	9	*c*	mr John McGeagh, in Peterhill
	10	*c*	mr william McCandlie, plantesion
	19		James Teatt, at the fforth Riuer, to his wife
	24	*c*	John boald, weauer

Agst	30	*c*	mr benjam Legg
	30	*c*	Alexr Mogerland, botcher
Sept	4	*c*	John McGlahlen
	10		Mr Moor in Caregfergos, pr Mrs Moor in Petér Hill
	21		James Mcmillen, in Melon [*Malone*]
	26		Thomas Seadge, pr mr William Ringland, Gowld Smith
	26	*c*	mr Joseph mcmun
	29	*c*	mr Georg Orr, Marinor
Oct	2		Wido Yeowart
	13	*w*	John ffife, Chanler in norstreat
	14	*c*	Charles Gardner, marinor, at the Slows bridg
	20		Samull mittchall, in norstret
	22	*w*	mosses Keain, marinor, pr mr John umpher, Scoallmaster
Nov	30		mr John Donelson, at Glenarm, pr mr James mcClure MarChant in Town
Desm	7		mr Kelsa, at the Rogh forth in Tampelpatrek peresh, pr mr John Howstan, Ealseler [*ale-seller*] in Town
	12		mr Philop bears, near belenie ffay [*Ballynafeigh*], Pr mr James Read, marChant in Town
	13	*w*	Allexr mcCay, in Keper [*innkeeper*], in Norstreat
	25	*c*	mr Thomas Whittsid, Ship Carpentar
	31		John mcelmen, at the Coaue hill, pr his ffather David mcelmnen
[1735]			
Janr	14	*c*	William Endslie, Glouer, in Rossemery Lean
	16	*c*	William Lasons, Smith, in Church Lean
ffebr	7	*b*	mr Joseph Innes, in Castelreah
	11		mr Gelbert mathies, in the ffales
	14	*w*	William Sttaford, marinor, pr his brother Allexr Sttaford
	15		mr Ross, of Portyvow, pr mr James mcClure
	16		Mrs bleair, in Town, pr mr John fforgeson, potegar [*apothecary*]
	16	*g*	mr James Wears, marinor, in ChurCh lean
	21	*w*	Lowes [*Lewis*] Shae, book binder
	25		Alexr park
mar	2	*c*	mr Hendrie wharton, Showmaker, in Curchlean [*Church Lane*].
	4	*m*	mr Alexr mcKeney, wine Copper with mr beggers Seler
	14	*s*	William Carson, breaklear, in Roossmery lean
	29	*c*	mr Joseph Potengar
Apr	4	*c*	mr William Lason, Smith, in Church-Lean
	12	*c*	Willm browne, Linnen Laper, at the whit hows
	14		mr James burdges ffather in Law, Liuing in bely Easton
	19		Hugh Doagh, at Tempelpatrek
	19	*c*	William Heanen, in norStreat
	26		mr James Whotel, in Lisburn, Pr mr James mcClure, MarChant, in Town
May	5	*w*	John Mean, in the plantesion
	16		mrs Harper, in Gleanarm, Pr mr James mcClure, in Town
Jun	2	*c*	mr Musentine, mar Chent, in Town
	5	*c*	Robart dowrie, Carperter, in nor-streat
	8		wido warkly, in Melon
July	4	*w*	mr Hugh Donnaldson, marChait, at the Stton bridg
	7	*s*	William Crue
			mr Ramsa, Shogerhouse
	16	*c*	James Rodgers, ship Carpenter
Agts	2	*c*	Haigh Kelley, weaver, harklous Lean
	11		William fforgeson, in Casel Reagh
	13	*w*	William Trallfor, in the ffalles
	19	*c*	James Paterson, in the Planttesion
	28	*w*	David wotherspon, Drumbo
Sept	4	*c*	Georg bell, weauer
	12		Robert brown, millwater
	22	*c*	mr John Ashmor, Glower
Octr	23		mr William Smith, in the Lope, Pr mr Smith, broad sttreat
	23	*c*	Angas waker, seaman
nor	1		James McDowald, Carrman, in the Plantesion
	26	*c*	John Ligget, in Long, weaver, for on of his ightbrs [*neighbour's*] Children
Desm			ye Reud mr bruse [*Rev. Michael Bruce, Holywood, died 1st Dec.*]

Desm 4 *c* Georg Endsly, Glouer
12 William mcCullogh, Taylor
16 *c* Andreew Townds
19 *c* John Clotworthie, far end of Church, brower, to mr Wallas
23 *c* Alexr Philleps, beaker
25 *w* John McCrakan, at Petershill

1735/6

Janr 3 *w* Alexander Mogerland, batcher
3 mrs Woods, at fowr lonends, Pr hir Doghter, mrs McGee, in Skepers Lean
5 *b* mr Samull McTear, in norstreat
14 *m* Mr James hameltoun Maxwel, at the Drumbridg
24 mr John Clugston, in Town, Pr sister mrs Elenar Clugston
28 mrs Elizabeth McCertnay, Pr mr Isaac McCertnay, MarChant

ffebr 12 *c* Alexr Mairs, Taylor, in Clugstons Entrie
13 *c* Alexr Mogerland, butcher
20 *m* mr Shawe, in beleygely

March 4 olld wido nickel, Pr hir Doghter, Doroty willson, in Ross marey Lean
27 *c* William McClearey, beaker, in Rossmery lean
29 the Reud mr Scoat, at Tampelpatreck
29 *w* mr Dallzel, the Carpenter
30 Mr James Ardbokels, Pr his son mr James Ardbokels

Apr 17 mr John Robeson, Pr mr Hugh Pringel, MarChant
14 A Coson of mr Innes, in The Town
28 *c* William Kenenan, Ship Carpenter, in Plantesion

May 8 *c* mr John vmphres, Scollmaster
9 *c* Robt streain, in Petershill
12 A brother son of mr Joseph Innes

Jun 5 *s* mr Whitsat, in bangor, Pr mr James mcClure, marchant
20 *c* David Layons, at stton bridg
29 Capt Craford.........Dunegor, Pr mr James burdges, marchent

July 4 ....Pr mr Daniel Mosentin.........
13 mr John Gregg in Gleneua, Pr his his son William Gregg in......stret
14 *w* James.........in Rogh forth in Tempelpatrek Parish
25 Mr John Alld, Marchent, in broad sttreat, Pr his wife

Agst 18 Mr James Weor (?), Marioner, Living in Church Lean
26 John Gregg, Junr, in Gleneua, Pr his brother William Gregg, scolar, in norstreat

Sept 2 *c* Alexr Thampson, Malster, norstreat
4 Antoney Thoborn, Marinor, Pr his wife
8 Mrs Teatt, Kirk Donel, Pr mr James mcClure
15 olld mr McKie, in banger, Pr his Gran son Reud mr McKie, minester in banger [*i.e., Rev. James Mackay, afterwards of First Belfast*]
22 *c* A brothers Child of mr Hugh Linn
24 mrs Ann brumly in Lurgan, Pr mr Hugh Pringel, MarChent
25 Thomas Spark, Carman, at Peter hill
28 *c* mr John Asmor
29 John mcCearts Mother in Law, in Peter hill

Octr 11 *w* Thomas Wason, Carpenter, in Millstreat
14 *c* Abrothers child of John Carter, in Peterhill
19 *c* Henery Coner, at the Pownd, weauer

[Here the Register ends.]

BIOGRAPHICAL NOTES

These notes on people mentioned in the register are prefaced by the text of the entry referring to them, and are arranged in chronological order of entry.

[1712 Jun-Jul]: the accounts at the end of the volume show that, among the lost entries on the first page, Samuel Smith senior paid for the funeral of Mr Catterwood, and John Shadges paid 'acct Mr Roan'.

1712 Jul 26 *mrs McBride*: the wife of the Rev. John McBride, presbyterian minister of Belfast. She was Margaret, daughter of William Fairlie of Tullyreevy and his wife, a niece of Gavin Hamilton of Killyleagh Castle. James Fairlie was her brother.

1712 Jul 29 *mr John Anderson Doctr* [add] pr Mrs Anderson widow (from notes at back of book).

1712 Aug 2 *mr Goudy*: Rev. John Goudy (1655-1733), presbyterian minister at Ballywalter from 1693, known as 'Goudy the prophet'.

1712 Jun 19 *mr John Shadgs, merchant*: he was the second son of Henry Chads the elder, a presbyterian merchant who was named as a burgess of Belfast in James II's charter of October 1688. Chades Bridge over the River Farset (which now runs under the High Street) was probably built by John's brother, Henry Chads junior, and was opposite the Cornmarket.

1712 Sep 6 *mrs Ann Buttle, pr Mr George*: George Buttle Conyngham was a son of the merchant David Buttle. He took the name Conyngham when he succeeded to the estates of his uncle William Conyngham of Springhill. Ann Buttle was his mother.

1712 Sep 13 *mr Ogilbe, Minister in Learn*: Rev. William Ogilvie, was presbyterian minister at Larne from 1700 and died 12 September 1712. He married a daughter of Patrick Agnew of Kilwaughter, high sheriff of Co. Antrim. The hire of his pall and cloaks cost £3 9s.

1712 Nov 30 *Doctr peacock, pr mr Sam Smith, Sener*: Dr John Peacock married Mary Upton, daughter of Arthur Upton of Castle Upton, Templepatrick, and widow of Dr Hugh Kennedy of Cultra. Their daughter Anne Peacock married George Buttle Conyngham (see above). The hire of the funeral gear cost £2 17s, of which £1 10s was eventually forgiven. Peacock died unexpectedly without making a will and had only time to tell Samuel Smith that he thought he had £500, which was to be divided equally among his three children. His son Upton Peacock was also a physician (see Benn, *History of Belfast*, p.576).

1713 Jan 20 *James Realy, Carpinter* [add] pr David fferguson, sexton

1713 Feb 17 *mr Heugh Boyde*: Hugh Boyd, merchant, father of Sarah Boyd, first wife of Samuel Smith, junior (see PRONI T828/21 for will).

1713 May 8 *Capt Stevenson*: probably Hans Stevenson of Killyleagh, M.P.

1713 May 26 *mrs Saffage, in New-Toun*: she was Mary Kennedy of Killearn, near Newtownards. Her first husband was Hans Hamilton of Carnasure, Comber, Co. Down (Hill, *The Montgomery Manuscripts*, p.185).

1713 Sep 6 *Hakens mccGill, Esqur*: John Hawkins Magill (c.1675-1713) assumed the name of Magill on succeeding to the estate of his maternal uncle, Sir John

Magill of Gill Hall, Co. Down (for Sir John's will, see PRONI D1594/71).

1713 Sep 15 *mrs Maxwell, at the Drum, pr mr William Rainey, juner*: presumably the first wife of Arthur Maxwell of the Drum.

1713 Dec 9 *mrs Addair at Loughan-More*: probably the widow of Benjamin Adair of Loughanmore. She was Ann, daughter of Walterhouse Crymble of Ballygallogh. She was presumably a descendant of Walterhouse (or Waterhouse) Crymble who was one of the original burgesses of Belfast, named in the charter of 1613. (For the Adairs of Loughanmore, see PRONI D3860.)

1713 Dec 11 *Margerat Laughling, pr Jas. ffrizell*: Frizell or Frissell is an old Belfast name which first appears in the freemen's roll in the 1660s. (For the freemen's roll, see Young, *The Town Book of Belfast*, pp.246-300.)

1714 Jan 13 *h mrs mccMinn*: Mrs McMinn was born Rose Stewart, daughter of James Stewart, merchant, of Belfast. She married first, in 1703, Andrew McMinn, merchant, (see PRONI D354/5-6 for their marriage articles), and second, Abel Hodgkis, nailer (see Registry of Deeds 44 462 30120).

1714 Jan 20 *mr William Martine*: probably youngest son of George Martin who was a burgess of Belfast, and sovereign 1649-50.

1714 Mar 17 *Lord Mussrain*: 3rd Viscount Massereene, born 1660, died 14 March 1714; married Rachel, daughter of Sir Edward Hungerford of Farley Castle, Somerset. The hire of funeral gear cost £2 11s.

1714 Apr 11 *Capt James Daben, at Dinnean*: The Dobbins are first noted at Carrickfergus in 1400 when Peter Dobbin was Constable of the Castle. The family subsequently acquired property in Counties Antrim and Down. They were divided in allegiance during the Williamite Wars, some of them serving in the Jacobite army. Captain James Dobbin of Duneane was 32 when he died. He was the son of William Dobbin, burgess of Belfast 1688-89, and his wife Mary Eccles. (For his tombstone, see *Memorials of the Dead*, VII, pp.514-15.)

1714 May 8 *c mr Robert Lennex*: Robert Lennox or Lenox was a Belfast merchant, and an elder of the First Rosemary Street Congregation. His daughter Anne married the Rev. Thomas Drennan and was the mother of Dr William Drennan.

1714 May 18 *mr John fforguson, poathicarrey* [add] 'c' for child

1714 Sep 19 *mrs Margerat Euless, pr mr John Blacke, Marchnt*: this should read Eccles not Euless. Black had married Jane Eccles, daughter of John Eccles of Malone.

1714 Dec 25 *mr David Buttle, pr Son George & mr William Cuningham*: David Buttle, a merchant of Belfast, became a burgess in 1700 and was sovereign 1702-03 and 1703-04. He resigned after the passing of the Test Act in 1704 which made it impossible for a presbyterian to hold the office of sovereign. He married Ann Conyngham, sister of William Conyngham of Springhill, Co. Londonderry, and was an ancestor of the Lenox-Conyngham family (see Mina Lenox-Conyngham, *An Old Ulster House and the People who lived in it* (Dundalk, 1946)).

1715 Apr 6 *mr Thos Poringer*: Thomas Pottinger, merchant of the staple of Belfast in 1664, was made sovereign during the Jacobite period by the charter of James II, 1688. He was said to have done much to protect lives and property during the Jacobite occupation of Belfast but was ousted when the previous sovereign and burgesses were restored. He was commissioner for prizes in Belfast 1691-97 and then lived for some years in London before returning in about 1709 to Belfast where he died, aged about 80.

1715 Apr 27 *c mr John Elsmor*: John Elsmore or Elsmere was a customs officer. He married Alice Bailie of Innishargy, half-sister of Sir Hans Sloane (for Sloane's career, see entry in the *Dictionary of National Biography*).

1715 Jun 15 *Capt Sam: Mountgomery*: a son of Hugh Montgomery of Ballymagoun, Co. Down.

1715 Jul 11 *mr Patterick Shaw*: probably Patrick Shaw of Dublin and British, Co. Antrim, a brother of John Shaw of Ballytweedy. He married Frances, daughter of William Shaw of Ganaway. The hire of his funeral equipment cost £3 15s. This is probably the most expensive funeral in the book as the rates went down at the end of the following year.

1715 Jul 12 *mr Thos Stewart, Ballidrean*: Thomas Stewart of Ballydrain, Co. Down, died 11 July 1715 aged 55, and was buried in Drumbeg Graveyard (see *Gravestone Inscriptions*, Co. Down, Vol. 3, p.29).

1715 Sep 5 *Mr ffreeland, Minister*: possibly the Rev. John Freeland, presbyterian minister at Killead, Co. Antrim, although he is said to have died on 12 March 1716.

1715 Dec 5 *Squr Dabb*: this must be one of the Dobbs family of Castle Dobbs. However, Richard Dobbs, who was mayor of Carrickfergus in 1690 and high sheriff of Co. Antrim, and who is most likely to have been described as 'Squire Dobbs', is generally said to have died in 1711.

1716 Apr 22 *cs mr Isaac MccCartiney*: Isaac Macartney was the younger son of Black George Macartney, a seventeenth century Belfast merchant. He was born in about 1670, was elected burgess in 1701 but resigned in 1707. He was also an elder of the First Rosemary Street Presbyterian Church. He was one of the leading merchants of his day and built, at his own expense, George Quay and Hanover Quay. He was eventually ruined and died in April 1738. This was an expensive funeral for a child. The hire of the pall and eight cloaks cost 14s 6d.

1716 Apr 24 *w mr John Mearss, Minister in New-town*: Rev. John Mairs, presbyterian minister at Newtownards from 1707, Moderator of the General Synod 1705, died 25 December 1718. He married Margaret Gilchrist in 1677.

1716 Jul 13 *w mr William Rainey, sener*: William Rainey senior, was a leading presbyterian merchant of Belfast. He had ten children, several of whom are noticed separately.

1716 Jul 14 *mr William Craford, pr son David*: William Craford or Crawford was a burgess of Belfast in 1686 and sovereign in 1692-93 and 1693-94, a founder member of the Second Rosemary Street Congregation, and M.P. for Belfast 1703-13. He purchased the Manor of Florida, Co. Down, which descended to the Gordon family through his granddaughter, Alice Arbuckle. (For his will, see Register of Deeds 17 37 8105.)

[1716 Jul] *mr Lason, pr mr John Euless, Marchnt*: Eccles not Euless

1716 Nov 10 *mr mccMulin, pr mr Hadock Esqur*: John McMullen of Dublin married Armanella Haddock at Lisburn on 11 August 1703. She was the sister of Roger Haddock of Carnbane, burgess 1708, and sovereign 1710-13.

1717 Jan 9 *Major Daben Dinnean*: Major John Dobbin of Duneane was at the siege of Londonderry in 1689, was a brother of William and Humphrey Dobbin, burgesses of Belfast 1688-89, and was aged 68 when he died (see *Memorials of the Dead*, VII, pp.514-5).

1717 Feb 14 *Lord Mount-alexdr*: the second earl was born 24 February 1650/1, died 12 February 1716/7 and was buried at Newtownards. He was succeeded in the earldom by his brother. The cost of hiring the funeral apparel was £1 14s. One of the cloaks was damaged and John Johnston the tailor was paid 1s 4d to mend it.

1717 May 28 *c mr James Blow*: James Blow and his brother-in-law Patrick Neill were Belfast's first printers. With the encouragement of the sovereign William Craford they set up the town's first printing press in about 1694. Neill died c.1705 and Blow in 1759 (see Benn, *History of Belfast*, pp.425-32).

1717 Jun 13 *mr patterick aDair, Minister at Carrickforguss*: born c.1675, presbyterian minister at Carrickfergus from 1702, died 12 June 1717.

1717 Nov 25 *mr John Rainey, pr Wife*: a merchant of Belfast and a member of the Second Rosemary Street Congregation. He was a son of William Rainey the elder and was born in 1669. His wife was Eleanor, daughter of John Galt the elder of Coleraine.

1718 Feb 8 *Alexdr Doliway Esqur*: Alexander Dallway was M.P. for Carrickfergus 1715-18.

1718 Mar 3 *mr John Tomb, Minister at Maherafelt*: presbyterian minister, married to Ann Martin, a granddaughter of George Martin who was sovereign in 1649-50. He was a brother-in-law of Francis Joy who married Ann Martin's sister. He died at Magherafelt on 28 February 1718.

1718 Mar 26 *mr Stafey petticrew*: Rev. Stafford Petticrew, minister at Ballyeaston from 1698.

1718 Mar 29 *mrs heterige, Widow, at Marherihall, pr mr Isaac MccCartiney*: the widow of the Rev. Matthew Haltridge, presbyterian minister of Ahoghill, who was the uncle of Isaac Macartney's wife.

1718 Apr 28 *mr John Knox at . . . per Son Thos*: this is John Knox of Ballycreely and Ringdufferin who was buried at Comber. He was a brother of Thomas Knox, M.P. for Dungannon and Privy Councillor. His son Thomas (1694-1769) was also M.P. for Dungannon and an ancestor of the Earls of Ranfurly.

1718 May 7 *Michall Bigger, Smith, pr Wife*: the numerous Belfast Biggers were descended from John, Michael, James and William Bigger or Biggar, Scottish merchants who settled in Belfast in the 1650s.

1718 Jun 12 *w mr John Chalmbers, Marchnt*: John Chalmers or Chambers, burgess from 1694 and sovereign in 1702, was married to a daughter of John Galt the elder, of Coleraine.

1718 Jul 2 *c mr John Mathers*: he was a former servant of John Chalmers, above. He married Chalmers's daughter Agnes in 1715 (see PRONI T1007/291).

1718 Jul 23 *Mr John MccBride*: born c.1651, educated at Glasgow, and became minister at Belfast in 1694. By his influence with the Earl of Donegall he obtained the lease of the site in Rosemary Lane, on which the meeting house was built in the early part of his ministry. He became a Non-Juror in1703 as he refused to take an oath that the Old Pretender was not the son of James II. He fled to Scotland and lived there from 1705-08, and again from 1711-14 (see entry in *Dictionary of National Biography*).

1718 Sep 3 *c Mr Daniel Musindin, Marchnt*: Daniel Mussenden was one of the leading merchants in Belfast in the first half of the eighteenth century. He purchased the Larchfield Estate between Lisburn and Ballynahinch, Co. Down, and died in 1763 (see PRONI D354 for his business papers).

1718 Nov 15 *Robert Holmes, in Skepers lean*: the Holmes family were in Belfast from the 1620s, most of them being ships' captains, mariners or merchants.

1718 Dec 29 *the Revd Mr ffillop Meares*: the register is misleading here, it was the Rev. Philip Mairs's father, the Rev. John Mairs, presbyterian minister at Newtownards, who was being buried. A note at the back of the volume states that Rev. Philip Mairs was charged 1s for bringing back the pall and cloaks as they were wanted for another funeral in Belfast on the same day.

1719 Mar 21 *Majer norie*: probably Nories or Norris

1719 Mar 23 *Mr Boyd, of the Glastry, pr Margret neven*: Thomas Boyd of Glastry, Co. Down (see PRONI T403/1 for his will dated 13 March 1718/19). Margaret Neven was probably his daughter.

1719 Mar 29 *c Mr James Cobame*: son of the Rev. Thomas Cobham of Dundonald and Holywood. He was born in 1678, was presbyterian minister at Broadisland from 1700, Moderator of General Synod in 1730, and died on 22 February 1759.

1719 May 22 *w Mr Hendrie Ealles, sufren* [add] pr Obadiah Groves: Henry Ellis became a burgess of Belfast in 1707 and sovereign in 1717, 1720 and 1722, dying in office. He was a lieutenant in the Army but lost his commission after killing his major in a duel. (For extracts from his will see Benn, *History of Belfast*, p.580.)

1719 Jun 4 *John Smith, poater, pr his wife*: the Belfast pottery was described in 1698: 'The new Pottery is a pretty curiosity, set up by Mr Smith, the present Sovereign, and his predecessor, Captain Leathes, a man of great ingenuity' [W. Sacheverall, *An Account of the Isle of Man*... (London, 1702), p.125]. John Smith the potter must have remarried because he buried a wife on 7 February 1713. The pottery which was on the north side of Waring Street was no longer operating after the 1720s.

1719 Jul 2 *pr Hugh Wales* [add] merchant

1719 Aug 4 *Mr John Greeg, in norstreat* [add] *pr his wife*; original reads 'Gregg'.

1719 Aug 20 *c Mr Bankes*: this is probably Thomas Banks, sovereign in 1729, who was Lord Donegall's agent. He married Elizabeth, daughter of John Montgomery, and was the father of Stewart Banks, sovereign of Belfast, Jane, who married John Black the younger of Bordeaux, and Catherine, who married William Macartney, M.P. for Belfast, who was Isaac Macartney's younger son.

1719 Oct 3 *Mr David Chalmers, MarChant*: the Chalmers family settled in Belfast in the seventeenth century. The first reference to them in the freemen's roll is to James Chalmers who became a merchant stapler in 1661, having served an apprenticeship in Belfast. There were several branches of the family and most of them were merchants or mariners. David Chalmers had an expensive funeral with the best pall and seventeen mourning cloaks. The sexton was paid 13s for ringing the church bell, the sovereign 10s for the ringing of the bell of the Market House (at the east side of the junction of the High Street and the Cornmarket) and a porter was paid 6d for sweeping the street for the funeral (see Benn, *History of Belfast*, p.581).

1719 Nov 5 *Cornl William Shaw, of the bosh*: Colonel William Shaw built the original seventeenth century house at The Bush in Co. Antrim. He played an active part in the Williamite Wars. 27 cloaks were hired for his funeral at a cost of £3 4s.

1719 Dec 2 *Mr Coalvien, in Dromor*: Rev. Alexander Colville the elder, presbyterian minister at Dromore, Co. Down, died suddenly in the pulpit on 1 December 1719.

1720 Jan 23 *Mr Allexr Chalmors, in peterhill*: Alexander Chalmers was an elder of the Third Congregation.

1720 Mar 30 *c Joarg Ashmor, Glover*: the Ashmores were one of the old Belfast families. The name first appears in the rating lists of 1639. The family were glovers and hatters for several generations.

1720 Mar 15 *wdd Ross, Scoullmistres . . . pr Mr Killpatricket*: Rev. James Kirkpatrick, a native of Scotland, was presbyterian minister at Templepatrick from 1699, and at Belfast from 1706, as colleague to the absent McBride. He was the first minister of the second meeting house which was built in 1708. He was a doctor of medicine as well as of divinity. He died in 1744 (see entry in *Dictionary of National Biography*).

1720 Mar 31 [add] m Will Delap, fellmaker, Norstreat

1720 Apr 15 *oJeam Campel*: should read Jean Campel, pr hir son John Campel

1720 Apr 22 for *Thubrow* read Thubron

1720 May 9 *wdd Adaire, in Caregforges*: probably widow of Rev. Patrick Adair. She was his cousin Isabel, grand-daughter of Sir Robert Adair, of Ballymena.

1720 May 21 *wdd watt, in Jolewood porish, pr hir son James wat, MarChent* [add] in Bridg Stret

1720 Jul 12 *Mr Blackwood, in bangwol*: John Blackwood of Ballyleidy, died 11 July 1720, buried in Bangor Abbey Graveyard (see *Gravestone Inscriptions*, Co. Down, Vol 17, p.20), ancestor of the Marquesses of Dufferin and Ava.

1720 Aug 14 *Mr Samull McClinton*: the McClinton or McClinto family were vintners.

1720 Aug 20 *w patr Crow, in peterhill*: should read 'brow' not 'Crow'. Patrick Brown was buried a week after his wife, on 27 August 1720.

1721 Jan 31 *David Stoormie, in belegomarten, pr William Stenson* [add] Peterhill

1721 Jan 31 *w John Gelston, in Cnoak parish*: Gelston's gravestone is in Knock Graveyard (see *Gravestone Inscriptions*, Co. Down, Vol 4, p.79).

1721 Feb *Wm Rainey, for Arthur Maxwell, Esq.*: Arthur Maxwell of the Drum, Co. Down, died on 22 January 1721, aged 74, having made a complicated will leaving his estate to a succession of nephews who had to take the name of Maxwell, the first being Captain James Hamilton Maxwell (see p. 55). The estate was eventually inherited by Arthur Rainey-Maxwell who was the son of William Rainey who had married Arthur Maxwell's niece (see PRONI D1255/3/3 for Maxwell's will, and *Gravestone Inscriptions*, Co. Down, Vol 3, p.23, for Maxwell's gravestone inscription in Drumbeg Churchyard). James Traill, who attended his funeral, wrote: 'he was a very rich man & loved ye things of ye world too much, but he had many valuable qualities & I hope he got into ye kingdom ofheaven' (see PRONI D1460/1).

1721 Apr 20 *Jno mcGlochlin* [add] taylor

1721 Jun 12 *Mr Cunnigham Esqr, in the Count of Dearey at Springhill*: William Conyngham of Springhill, Co. Londonderry, married Anne, daughter of Arthur Upton of Castle Upton, Templepatrick, Co. Antrim, in 1680. In his will (PRONI D1449/1/33) he stipulated that not more than £50 was to be spent on his funeral.

The hire of funeral gear cost only £1 16s. He died childless leaving his estates to his nephew George Buttle, son of David Buttle, sovereign of Belfast. George, who took the name of Conyngham, was an ancestor of the Lenox-Conyngham family (see Mina Lenox-Conyngham, *An Old Ulster House, and the People who lived in it* (Dundalk, 1946)).

1721 Nov 8 *Madom paotenger, in Careforgous*: the widow of Captain Edward Pottinger, brother of Thomas (see p. 44). Edward was a sea captain and a burgess of Belfast under James II's charter of 1688. After Schomberg's invasion he became a naval captain in command of the *Dartmouth* with two other ships under his orders. The *Dartmouth* sheltered from a storm in the Sound of Mull but was driven on to a rocky island. Pottinger and all but six of the crew of about 130 were lost. The remains of the ship were discovered in 1973 and excavated. Pottinger's widow was a daughter of Solomon Faith of Carrickfergus by his wife Catherine Dobbin. Captain James Maxwell Hamilton was one of her sons-in-law.

1721 Nov 10 *the Colectors leady*: the Collector of Customs at Belfast was George Macartney (1671-1757), M.P. for Belfast 1715-57. His lady was his first wife Letitia, daughter and co-heiress of Sir Charles Porter, Lord Chancellor of Ireland.

1721 Nov 30 [add] w Robt Sinklar Shomaker pr Geo Carson

1722 Jan 2 *s Rev. Mr Mckraken, in lesburn*: Rev. Alexander McCracken, presbyterian minister at Lisburn from 1688, refused to take the Oath of Abjuration and was imprisoned at Carrickfergus 1713-16. He died 14 November 1730.

1722 Jan 3 *Mr Orr in Combar* [add] pr his Clark Will Gambel: Rev. Thomas Orr, presbyterian minister at Comber from 1695, was Moderator of the General Synod from 1709, and died 1 January 1722.

1722 Jan 10 *c Mrs Smith, in the Shogerhovs, pr hir son John:* omit 'c' for child.

1722 Jan 11 *Mr briss blear, pr John fforgeson*: Brice Blair, bookseller and haberdasher, and elder, was agent for the distribution of the Regium Donum from 1708. (The Regium Donum was an annual grant by the Crown for the support of presbyterian ministers.)

1722 Jan 28 *William Gaieit*: spelt 'Galt' in the elders' notes

1722 Feb 23 *Mr Talford*: Nicholas Thetford, merchant and chandler, was a burgess of Belfast from 1708. He refused to accept election in 1707 when the presbyterian burgesses were ousted, not wanting a burgess-ship 'coming in such a manner' (see Young, *Town Book of Belfast*, p.236).

1722 Mar 16 *s the Revd mr Mccapien*: Rev. James McAlpine conducted a Philosophical School at Killyleagh 1697-1714. He was presbyterian minister at Ballynahinch, married Isabel Hamilton, and died 27 October 1732.

1722 Apr 8 *John Haselton, Elder, pr his wife*: he left two alms dishes to the two meeting houses in Belfast.

1722 May 9 *olld Mr Reanney*: this is William Rainey the elder, a presbyterian merchant of Belfast. He was born in 1639 or 1640 at Whitehouse, Co. Antrim, the son of John Rainey (1602-82). His brothers were Robert Rainey of Killybegs, whose grand-daughter Grizzel married Robert Joy of Belfast, and Hugh Rainey of Magherafelt who endowed a charity school there. William had a large family including William Rainey the younger.

1722 May 30 *s wdd Campbel*: this entry indicates that there were guilds or trade organisations in Belfast at this date.

1722 Jul 13 *brown Gorge McCartnay*: Brown George was a presbyterian merchant who became a freeman in 1681, having served his apprenticeship in Belfast. His exact relationship to the Macartneys of Lissanoure and of Blacket is unknown.

1722 Aug 6 *Mr Robert Andrew, MarChant, pr his son Gebrall*: his son and heir was called Gabriel. He left goods and property worth £2360 1s 2½d (see PRONI T283B p.29 for his will).

1722 Aug 8 *Mrs Ann Martin, pr Mr ffransess Joy (son in law)*: the words 'son-in-law' are an addition, possibly written over an erasure. The words may not be in the same hand as the rest of the page but were written in the eighteenth century as 'son' is written with a long 's'. The information is, in fact, incorrect. Francis Joy's mother-in-law was Catherine Martin and Ann Martin was her cousin (see Joy MSS at Linen Hall Library).

1722 Sep 20 *Mr John Kennedy of Coltra*: probably son of Dr Hugh Kennedy, of Cultra, Co. Down, and his wife Mary, daughter of Arthur Upton. He married Martha, daughter of William Stewart of Ballylawn, Co. Down.

1722 Nov 3 *Mr Edward Whitloack*: [add] c for child.

1722 Dec 22 *c Mr boyd, of the Gleasrie*: this is Glastry, Co. Down.

1723 Feb 3 *Dauid beggs, Carman* [add] for his wife

1723 Mar 23 *Capt Treall, pr Joseph Podgenar*: Patrick Traill of Sanday, in the Orkneys, married Esther, daughter of Thomas Pottinger and sister of Joseph Pottinger. Under Scottish law this marriage was bigamous (see Sir James Fergusson, *The White Hind and other Discoveries* (London, 1963), pp.114-25).

1723 May 19 *Alexr Mcmun*: a presbyterian merchant and brother of John McMunn.

1723 Jun 5 *w Mr Roase, Lodge*: written elsewhere in the volume as Ross.

1723 Aug 31 *Mr William MuntGomry pr his wife*: William Montgomery was a son of the merchant John Montgomery and a brother-in-law of Thomas Banks (see PRONI T1860/13 for his will).

1723 Sep 9 *w Mr Stoward Esqr, Celey mon*: the Stewart family were landed gentry living at Killymoon, Cookstown, Co. Tyrone.

1723 Oct 28 *olld Doctor fforgeson*: Dr Victor Ferguson was a presbyterian and an elder of the Second Rosemary Street Congregation. Captain McCulloch was his son-in-law.

1723 Nov 9 c *Mr will Leg, in Mellon*: William Legg of Malone married, first, Mary Eccles, and second, Eleanor Graham, both of whom are buried in Drumbeg Churchyard (see *Gravestone Inscriptions*, Co. Down, Vol. 3, p.17).

1723 Dec 8 *Mr John yowng, MarChant* [add] per Mr Alexr

1723 Dec 24 *c Mr Joarg McCartnay*: there were several George McCartneys in Belfast at this date. This George was probably a son of Brown George McCartney. His wife was the daughter and heiress of Thomas Knox of Belfast, a cousin of Thomas Knox of Dungannon.

1723 Dec 25 *warham Smith*: probably Warham Smith, whitesmith of Dublin, son of Simon Smith of the Lodge, parish of Belfast (see Registry of Deeds 21 122 10963).

1724 Jan 27 *w Robt Lawe* [add] Norstreat

1724 Feb 5 *the Leat Sr John Roding*: Sir John Rawdon, born 1690, M.P. for Co. Down 1717-24, married Dorothy Levinge, died 2 February 1724. He was an ancestor of the Earls of Moira and Marquesses of Hastings. 24 cloaks were hired for his funeral.

1724 Feb 28 *the Leatt Revd Mr Sam getty in learn, pr Mr gebrall Andreow*: Rev. Samuel Getty, presbyterian minister at Larne from 1715, died 27 February 1724. Gabriel Andrews's mother was probably a Getty.

1724 Mar 2 *m Mr John Clarke, the MarChent* [add] pordis born (i.e. Purdysburn, Co. Down)

1724 Mar 8 *the Leat Revd Mr Williamson, in belenhinch*: Rev. John Williamson, M.A., vicar of Magheradroll (Ballynahinch) from 1694.

1724 Apr 15 *c the Revd Mr Harper*: Rev. Samuel Harper or Harpur, presbyterian minister at Moira from 1717, died 1731

1724 Jul 12 *Mr Jon Mcmun, MarChent*: John McMunn, a presbyterian merchant, was the brother of Alexander McMunn and treasurer of the First Congregation from 1717.

1724 Aug 30 *w yowng Samull Smith, MarChent*: Smith's first wife Sarah was a daughter of Hugh Boyd (see p. 43). His second wife was Ann Galt by whom he was the father of John Galt Smith (1731-1802), one of leading Belfast merchants in the eighteenth century (see *Gravestone Inscriptions*, Belfast, Vol. 4, p.151).

1724 Sep 20 *Mr David black, Pr his father Mr Jon black, fowr Corners*: David was a brother of John Black the elder of Bordeaux. Four Corners was the junction of Waring Street, Bridge Street, North Street and Rosemary Lane.

1724 Oct 8 *c Edwar Harie*: probably Haries or Harris.

1724 Dec 1 *Mr Agnew of Celwaghter*: Patrick Agnew of Kilwaughter, Co. Antrim.

1724 Dec 29 *Mrs Gresell Reney, Pr Mr Jon Ecels*: Grissell Rainey (1678-1724) was an unmarried daughter of William Rainey the elder. John Eccles was her brother-in-law.

1725 Jan 15 *Isack Ramige, Carman, Pr Charels Rainge* [i.e. Ramage]: the first member of this family to appear in the Belfast freemen's roll was Henry Ramage, porter, in 1680. The family were in business as carriers.

1725 Feb 6 *the Leat Squeair Hatreckt*: John Haltridge was a burgess of Belfast from 1707, M.P. for Killyleagh, and high sheriff of Co. Down in 1699. He was the only son of William Haltridge of Dromore, a wealthy merchant, and, although from a presbyterian family, he was a member of the Church of Ireland. He had no surviving heirs and left his encumbered estates in Counties Down and Armagh to his brother-in-law Isaac Macartney, thereby contributing to Macartney's financial problems. Haltridge married (1699) Grace, daughter of Sir William Sands of Co. Kildare. After his death she remarried twice, and died 2 January 1728.

1725 Feb 11 *f Mr Capt Maxwell* [add] Hamelton: Captain James Maxwell Hamilton's father was Archibald Hamilton who died on 9 February 1725 aged 80, and is buried in Drumbeg Churchyard (see *Gravestone Inscriptions*, Co. Down, Vol.3, p.14). Captain James was also known as Hamilton Maxwell.

1725 Feb 20 *Mr Cromie, High Shieref*: Ezekiel William Crombie of Cromore, high sheriff of Co. Antrim.

1725 Feb 26 *c Adam Patey, planteson* [add] pr Mr Robert Thomason

1725 Mar 12 *c Edward whitloack, Mar Chent*: the Whitlocks or Whitelocks were another old Belfast family. A John Whitelock appears in the rating list for 1639. Many of the family were butchers.

1725 Mar 24 *m olld Sam Smith, living in Dunegoar, Pr Mr Pat Smith*: a note in another part of the volume indicates that she was Patrick Smith's grandmother.

1725 Jun 29 *Mrs Maxwel, of Obeday Groaues, of ffiney broag*: she was the second wife of Henry Maxwell of Finnebroage, Co. Down, whom he married in 1713 (see PRONI D1556/16/3 for her marriage settlement). She was Dorothy Brice, daughter of Colonel Edward Brice of Kilroot, an eminent merchant of Belfast.

1725 Jul 1 *Joarg Jhnston, Barber, in Mill streat*: it was his wife's funeral.

1725 Jul 9 *c Mr Jon McCartney*: John McCartney was a son of Brown George McCartney, and like his father was a merchant. He married a daughter of Alexander Dallway, M.P. for Carrickfergus.

1725 Aug 15 *Mr John Challmbrs, MarChent, Pr his son James*: John Chalmers was a presbyterian merchant who was a burgess in 1688-89, and from 1693, and was sovereign 1701-02.

1725 Sep 5 *c Mr Edr burt, sufron in town*: the Byrtt or Le Byrtt family came from Carrickfergus. Nathaniel Byrtt was one of the new Church of Ireland burgesses elected in 1707 and was sovereign in 1725, dying in his year of office.

1725 Oct 13 *Mr William Smith, Pr his brother Mr John Smith, Shogerhouse*: William and John Smith were sons of Captain David Smith, burgess and sovereign of Belfast, and ran the Belfast sugar refinery after his death (see PRONI T455/1).

1725 Nov 8 *Mr William Raney, MarChant*: William Rainey the younger, merchant of Belfast, was born in North Street, Belfast, in 1671. His first wife was Jane, daughter of Alderman Edward Brooke of Londonderry. He married secondly Katherine Shaw, niece of Arthur Maxwell of the Drum (see p. 48). He died of a fever at 8 o'clock on the morning of 6 November (see PRONI D2092/1/2/101).

1725 Nov 28 *c Robart Thomson, ship Carpenter, plantesion*: delete 'c'.

1725 6 *wdd Granger* [add] Dec

1726 Jan 12 *c Caluen Darlen* [add] barber

1726 Feb 14 *c Cornall Edward brise, who was boried in Balleycarey*: Colonel Edward Brice was a grandson of the Rev. Edward Brice (1569-1636), Prebendary of Kilroot. He was a brother of Randal Brice, M.P. for Lisburn, and of Mary Brice who married Thomas Knox of Dungannon. He died in 1742 at the age of 83. By his second marriage he was ancestor of the Bruce family of Kilroot. The child who died was a two year old girl and Brice's brother-in-law, Arthur Dobbs, wrote 'my brother Brice has lost his hopeful girl for which he and my sister grieves excessively' (see PRONI D2092/1/2/85).

1726 Apr 17 *Mr Jno black, Pr Mr James Arbockels*: John Black, merchant of Belfast, was born in 1647. His son John established himself as a wine merchant in Bordeaux and had a numerous family including Dr Joseph Black, the chemist and philosopher. John Black the elder was an apprentice of Thomas Pottinger. He married Jane Eccles, a daughter of John Eccles of Malone who entertained King William III in 1690 (see Benn, *History of Belfast*, pp.268-9). She was a sister of Sir John Eccles, Mayor of Dublin. James Arbuckle was Black's son-in-law, having married his daughter Priscilla in 1706.

1726 May 10 *Mrs Arther, at the fowr Corners, Pr hir Granson, Arther Burt*: Arthur Byrtt, burgess 1729 and many times sovereign of Belfast.

1726 Jun 23 *c Mr Maxwel, of ffeney Broag, Pr Corn Brise in Town*: Henry Maxwell's second wife was Dorothy, daughter of Col. Edward Brice. This child was presumably one of Brice's grandchildren.

1726 Jun 23 *b Mrs Clogstan*: the Clugstons emigrated to Belfast from south-west Scotland in the 1630s. Several members of the family were merchants in the mid seventeenth century and they left numerous descendants.

1726 Aug 20 *olld Mr James Smith, Pr his son James, norStreat*: Old James Smith was a maltman (see PRONI T808/13415 for his will). His son James was buried on 31 December in this year.

1727 Jan 22 *Mr John Eacles, MarChant, in broad streat*: John Eccles, married (1693) Jane Rainey, daughter of William Rainey the elder. They had no children so he left his property to the children of his brother Hugh Eccles (see PRONI T581/4, p.302).

1727 3 [March] *Mrs becerStaf* [add] Mar

1727 May 20 *s Parson Hamelton, in banger*: probably Rev. Robert Hamilton, vicar of Bangor. The funeral was of a sister not a son.

1727 Jul 15 *Mr Ritchard Ashmor, hatter, in mell Streat* [add] pr his mother

1727 Aug 9 *s John hamelton*: this was his sister not his son.

1727 Aug 28 c *mr James bigger* [add] merchant

1727 Sep 11 *mrs Clugston, Pr hir son the sofren*: she was the widow of Robert Clugston who died c.1711. The sovereign was their son, John Clugston.

1727 Oct 25 *mr William Arbuckel*: son of James Arbuckle and Priscilla Black. He married the daughter of William Craford, M.P.

1728 Sep 20 *olld Madam Dalaway*: probably the widow of Alexander Dallway, M.P for Carrickfergus.

1729 Jan 4 *mr John McCartnay, marClent, Pr the Revd mr Samull Helleday*: a son of Brown George McCartney. His wife Elizabeth was the daughter of Alexander Dallway, M.P. for Carrickfergus. The Rev. Samuel Haliday was called to Belfast 1719 and installed 1720. The opposition to his installation, without subscription, led to the founding of the Third Congregation, Belfast, and to the formation of the Antrim Presbytery (see entry for Haliday in the *Dictionary of National Biography*). Haliday married Elizabeth McCartney's aunt who was the widow of Arthur Maxwell of the Drum, and died 5 March 1739.

1729 Apr 2 *w Doacter Smith in town*: if this is Dr Andrew Smith, his wife was a daugh ter of John Chalmers, merchant (see Register of Deeds 54 366 36082).

1729 May 1 *Iserell Coates, Liung in the falles*: the Coates family held land in the Falls since at least the 1640s. Israel married a daughter of John Eccles of Malone (see T581/3 p.59 for Eccles's will).

1729 May 3 *Thomas ffeares, Sealler, his mother in Lawe* [add] in Millstreat

1729 May 20 *the Reud mr John Mallcom, in Dun morey*: Rev. John Malcom, was presbyterian minister at Dunmurry from 1699, and died 17 May 1729 (see entry in the *Dictionary of National Biography*).

1729 Aug 29 *Olld Madam Pottenger, Pr hir son mr Joseph Pottenger*: she was the widow of Thomas Pottinger who died in 1715.

1729 Sep 7 c mr *William mcCaulie*: possibly McCanlie

1729 Dec 13 *olld mrs Craford, Pr hir son Dauid*: she was the widow of William Craford, M.P. for Belfast, who died in 1716.

1730 Feb 24 *the Revd mr James bruse, Keleleah*: Rev. James Bruce, born 1661, was the son of Rev. Michael Bruce of Killinchy, presbyterian minister at Killyleagh from 1687, and died 17 February 1730.

1730 Nov 17 *mr Georg Manken, at the millwater* [add] pr his son Thomas: the Mankins were one of the oldest Belfast families. They first appear in the rating lists for the 1640s.

1731 Jan 3 *w Mr Arther Tattford, pr the Revd Mr Neclous Tatford*: Arthur Thetford became a burgess in 1729. He married Esther, daughter of William Rogers, merchant of Belfast, in 1726 (see Registry of Deeds 63 137 42968 for their marriage articles). He and the Rev. Nicholas Thetford were sons of Nicholas Thetford, burgess of Belfast, who died in 1722.

1731 Jan 7 *the Reud mr Sinklear*: Rev. Robert Sinclair, presbyterian minister at Islandmagee from 1704, died 5 January 1731.

1731 Mar 19 *Doacter Cromie, Pr his brother in Law Mr John magenis, Liuing besids Drummor*: Dr George Cromie, a physician, was the son of Francis Cromie, merchant of Dublin, and his wife Alice, sister of Isaac Macartney. His sister Maria (Molly) Cromie married John Magenis of Shanrod, near Dromore. Her will was proved in 1765 and she was buried in the Cromie family burying ground at St Michan's, Dublin (see PRONI T185/14).

1731 Jul 8 *s mr Georg maCertney Esqr*: George Macartney Esq., M.P. for Belfast, was the grandfather of Earl Macartney. This son who died was called Hugh.

1731 Jul 15 *neas of Toallen*: this could be read as To allen or Jo allen.

1731 Aug 12 *Robert ffisher, in the ffalles* [add] pr Mr Bankes

1731 Nov 3 *d widdo Agnew, at Cewaghter*: probably a daughter of Patrick Agnew of Kilwaughter who died in 1724.

1731 Dec 6 *Mr ffranses Cromie, Pr mr James bllow*: Francis Cromie, a son of the Dublin merchant William Cromie, was the son-in-law of the Belfast printer, James Blow. Blow's daughter then married the printer George Grierson as his second wife (see Benn, *History of Belfast*, p.431).

1732 Aug 7 *Maigor upton, in tampelpatrek*: Hercules Upton was one of the sons of Arthur Upton of Castle Upton.

1732 Aug 8 *s the Reved mr wolson, in beley Clair*: Rev. Thomas Wilson, presbyterian minister at Ballyclare from 1711, died 1767.

1732 Sep 13 [add] c Thomas whittsid, on the kee

1732 Nov 16 *mr Gabriel Andrews, MarChent, Pr his brother Hugh Andrews*: sons of Robert Andrews (see p. 50)

1732 Dec 22 *s Rev. Mr Clugston, in Larn*: the Rev. Josias Clugston died aged 80 on 10 August 1775 and is buried in Larne Churchyard.

1732 Dec 25 *mrs Potter, mother in Law to Robart Armstrong, marChent in town, whos mother in Law Liued in Kelenchie*: she was the wife of John Potter, merchant of Killinchy, who died 1746. She died 23 December 1732 aged 70. Robert Armstrong was married to their daughter Abigail (see *Gravestone Inscriptions*, Co. Down, Vol. 4, p.40).

1733 Jan 15 *mr James Challmbrs, marioner* [add] to his wife

1733 Mar 5 *mrs mcCullogh at Shaes bridg, Pr mr Dauid Craford, in Town*: probably David Craford's aunt. His father William Craford, M.P., named his sister Grissel McCullogh in his will and left her an annuity of £4 (see Register of Deeds 17 37 8105).

1733 Mar 26 *Harcoles mcGomrie, Esqr in beley Leson, Drumbo*: Hercules Montgomery of Ballylesson, married a daughter of the Rev. Archibald McNeil, Chancellor of the Cathedral of Down.

1733 Jun 4 *c wido Arbockels, in Rosse marey Lean, Pr olld mrs Ardbockels*: wido Arbockels was Anne, widow of William Arbuckle. Old Mrs Arbuckle was probably her husband's grandmother who was buried in the following September.

1733 Jun ?29 [add] c David Layon, ventner

1733 Dec 23 [add] Sam McDowald at ye browrie

1733 Dec 23 [should read Dec 27] *Widdo McDowald, at ye brurie*

1734 Jan 17 *mr Andrew Kelsay, in the Roghforth, in Tampolpatrook Peresh* [add] pr Mr Sam Mittchall in norstreat, marchant

1734 Apr 14 *Arthur Graye* [add] 'w' for wife

1734 May 2 *ye Revd mr Taylor, in Carn Castel*: Rev. William Taylor, presbyterian minister at Cairncastle from 1715, married Mary Latimer, and died 2 May 1734.

1734 May 8 *Mr David Craford*: the only surviving son and heir of William Craford, M.P., who died in 1716. David inherited the Manor of Florida, Co. Down. He was married to Mary Hamilton of Dunamangh, Co. Tyrone. (For his will see PRONI T700 p.55.)

1734 Aug 3 *Doacter mcneall, pr mr Archbald mcneall*: probably Neal McNeale, presbyterian burgess of Belfast 1703-07, variously described as apothecary, doctor and gentleman. Archibald McNeale was his nephew.

1734 Sep 21 *James Mcmillen*: should read McMullen

1734 Sep 26 *Thomas Seadge*: Thomas Chads, one of the sons of Henry Chads the elder, burgess of Belfast 1688-89.

1734 Sep 26 *c mr Joseph mcmun* [add] per his mother Mrs McMunn. Joseph was a son of the presbyterian merchant Alexander McMunn.

1734 Oct 20 *Samull mittchall, in norstret* [add] pr his wife

1734 Oct 22 [add] c Thomas Qua, polster

1734 Dec 7 *mr Kelsa, at the Rogh forth . . .* [add] 's' for son

1734 Dec 25 c *mr Thomas Whittsid, Ship Carpentar* [add] on the Kee: the Whitesides had been in Belfast since the 1640s.

1735 Mar 29 *c mr Joseph Potengar*: Joseph Pottinger, son of Thomas Pottinger, married Mary Dunlop.

1735 Apr 19 *Hugh Doagh, at Tempelpatrek*: the Doake family are found in the rating lists of the 1640s. The most notable member of the family was Hugh Doake, burgess 1645-69, and sovereign 1647-48.

1735 Jun 5 *c Robart dowrie*: should read Lowrie

1735 Dec *ye Reud mr bruse*: Rev. Michael Bruce, eldest son of Rev. James Bruce of Killyleagh, presbyterian minister at Holywood from 1711, died 1 December 1735 aged 46, buried in Holywood Graveyard.

1736 Jan 14 *m Mr James hameltoun Maxwel, at the Drumbridg*: his mother was Margaret, widow of Archibald Hamilton, died 12 January 1736 aged 85, buried in Drumbeg Churchyard (see *Gravestone Inscriptions*, Co. Down, Vol. 3, p.14). She was a sister of Arthur Maxwell of the Drum.

1736 Jan 24 *mr John Clugston, in Town, Pr sister mrs Elenar clugston*: John Clugston, sovereign for several terms between 1726 and 1733.

1736 Jan 28 *mrs Elizabeth McCertnay, Pr mr Isaac McCertnay, MarChant*: Isaac Macartney's unmarried sister. Their father was the merchant Black George Macartney, burgess from 1665, and four times sovereign.

1736 Mar 29 *the Reud mr Scoat, at Tampelpatreck*: probably Rev. Hugh Scott, born at Templepatrick, presbyterian minister of Killead 1733, and of Newtownards Non-Subscribing Congregation from 1735, died 27 March 1736.

1736 Mar 30 *Mr James Ardbokels, Pr his son mr James Ardbokels*: James Arbuckle the elder married Priscilla, daughter of John Black. James Arbuckle the younger married Mary Lutwidge and died on the Isle of Man in 1739 (see *Belfast Newsletter*, 1 May 1739).

1736 Sep 15 *olld mr McKie in banger, Pr his Gran son Reud mr McKie, minester in banger*: Rev. James Mackay, born 1709, presbyterian minister of Bangor 1732, removed to Clonmel 1740, installed at Belfast 1756, died 22 January 1781.

INDEX

9 780901 905673

www.ingramcontent.com/pod-product-compliance
Lightning Source LLC
Chambersburg PA
CBHW080255030426
42334CB00023BA/2823